PENGUIN CLASSICS

THE SHATTERED THIGH

BHASA is a celebrated name in classical Sanskrit drama. Although his dates have not been conclusively established, it is certain that he preceded Kalidasa, who has praised him by name in the prologue of one of his own plays. It has been suggested that Bhasa lived in the Mauryan period, the fourth or the third century BC, but most scholarly opinion places him in the first or the second century AD.

Bhasa's plays were lost over a period of time but thirteen were rediscovered in Kerala at the beginning of the twentieth century. Of these six, forming the present collection, are based on the *Māhābhārata* story which Bhasa embellished for obtaining dramatic effects. The remaining seven are derived from the *Rāmāyana*, the *Harivamśa* and legends and stories prevalent at the time.

Bhasa wrote in a period which was politically, socially, economically and most importantly, culturally dynamic. Theatre was already an established art form and the foremost treatise on fine arts, Bharata's *Nātyaśāstra*, was written in the same period. Plays were written and performed by professionals supported by other well-developed aspects of stagecraft.

For over fifteen hundred years classical Indian commentators and anthologists have counted Bhasa among the foremost writers of ancient India. He made use of the Sanskrit language in a simpler form as compared to the more ornate style of later playwrights. He dispensed with the opening benediction or *nāndi* and began his plays directly with the stage direction. And, most importantly, he broke with convention by giving a tragic ending to one of his plays, *Urubhangam*, with the death of the hero on stage.

*

ADITYA NARAYANA DHAIRYASHEEL HAKSAR was born in Gwalior and educated at the Doon School and the universities of Allahabad and Oxford. A well-known translator of Sanskrit classics, he has also had a distinguished career as a diplomat, serving as Indian high commissioner to Kenya and the Seychelles, minister to the United States, and ambassador to Portugal and Yugoslavia. Haksar's translations from the Sanskrit include *Hitopadesa, Simhasana Dvatrimsika, Tales of the Ten Princes* and *Subhashitavali*, all published as Penguin Classics. He has also compiled *A Treasury of Sanskrit Poetry*.

THE SHATTERED THIGH
And Other Plays

BHASA

Translated from the original Sanskrit
with an Introduction by
A.N.D. HAKSAR

PENGUIN BOOKS
An imprint of Penguin Random House

PENGUIN BOOKS

USA | Canada | UK | Ireland | Australia
New Zealand | India | South Africa | China | Singapore

Penguin Books is part of the Penguin Random House group of companies whose addresses can be found at global.penguinrandomhouse.com

Published by Penguin Random House India Pvt. Ltd
4th Floor, Capital Tower 1, MG Road,
Gurugram 122 002, Haryana, India

Penguin Random House India

First published by Penguin Books India 1993
This edition published 2008

10 9 8 7 6 5 4 3 2

ISBN 9780143104308

Typeset by Eleven Arts, Delhi

Printed at Manipal Technologies Limited, India

www.penguin.co.in

FSC www.fsc.org MIX Paper | Supporting responsible forestry FSC® C043100

This is a legitimate digitally printed version of the book and therefore might not have certain extra finishing on the cover.

P. M. S.

For
B.
with love
on her birthday

Contents

Introduction to the New Edition

An eminent contemporary scholar of Sanskrit literature has expressed the view that Bhasa's plays, with their comparative brevity, rapid incident-filled action and dramatic changes, 'seem to have an eye to the stage rather than to a reader.'* A well known modern playwright says that 'every line in these texts is actable . . . the gesture behind each word is clearly visible even on the printed page.'†

Without detracting in any way from the readability of Bhasa's work, these comments on its actability are particularly applicable to the *Mahābhārata* plays of this great dramatist of ancient India. Part of the living *Kutiyattam* tradition of Kerala, included in the syllabus of the National School of Drama, Bhasa has been produced in various Indian languages and also in the original Sanskrit. Records of production in English are scanty, but plays from the present translation have been reported§ as staged and lauded since their first publication more than a decade ago.

The credit for bringing out this new edition goes to Ravi Singh, Publisher and Editor-in-Chief of Penguin India. My thanks to him, and to R. Sivapriya and Paromita Mohanchandra for the consequential practical arrangements. This has also given me the opportunity to make a few corrections.

Noida A.N.D.H.
5 October 2007

*A.K. Warder, *Indian Kavya Literature*, Vol. II, Delhi, 1974.
†Girish Karnad, *The Book Review*, Delhi, October, 1993.
§Barbara Williams, *The Peoples Review* (Online Edition), April 25–May 1, 2002.

Introduction

Bhasa is a celebrated name in classical Sanskrit literature. The figure best known today from what remains of that literature, which once pervaded the entire South Asian subcontinent and beyond, is of course Kalidasa. In the prologue of his play, *Mālavikāgnimitram*, that great poet and dramatist of ancient India poses the following question: 'How can the work of the modern poet Kalidasa be more esteemed than the works of Bhasa, Kaviputra, Saumillaka and others of established fame?'[1] An impeccable answer follows in the next line: 'Everything is not praiseworthy, just because it is old; nor should a poetical work be dismissed just because it is new.' But this brief dialogue makes it clear that Bhasa was already well known on the Indian literary scene over fifteen hundred years ago, when Kalidasa had just begun to make his mark.

Two hundred years later, the classical period was in its last phase. Bhasa remained well known across the country. In North India, Bana Bhatta, the first Sanskrit novelist and the court-poet of King Harsha in seventh century Kanauj, has this to say in his biography of the king, *Harshacharita*: 'Bhasa earned fame by his plays which commenced with the producer, had many roles, and were (grand) like temples with banners.'[2] And in South India, Dandin, the critic and prose stylist from Kanchi of the same century, writes in his *Avantisundarikathā* that even though departed, Bhasa lives on, embodied in his plays with their craftsmanship.

Six hundred years nearer the present time, Bhasa, Kalidasa and Bana are included in an oft-quoted tribute to poets of yore by Jayadeva in his thirteenth century work, *Prasanna Rāghava*. 'Who will not delight in the Muse of Poetry,' asks the writer, 'the lovely maid whose laughter is Bhasa, the guru of poets, whose sport of pleasure is Kalidasa, whose Cupid is Bana . . .?'[3]

Bhasa is also mentioned in other medieval works: in Vakpatiraja's eighth century Prakrit poem *Gauda Vaho*; in the Sanskrit literary critiques, Rajasekhara's *Kāvya Mimāmsa* and Ramachandra's *Nātya Darpana*, of the tenth and twelfth centuries respectively; and in the verse anthologies *Sūktimuktāvali*, *Śārngadhara Paddhati* and *Subhāshitāvali*, compiled respectively in Maharashtra, Rajasthan and Kashmir in the thirteenth, fourteenth and fifteenth centuries. In the second of these, in a stanza ascribed to the famous tenth century critic Rajasekhara, Bhasa heads a list of sixteen ancient writers, including names like Kalidasa and Bharavi, who had mastered the Goddess of Speech.[4] In the first anthology a quotation from the same critic names and lauds one of Bhasa's plays.[5]

The three anthologies also contain some stanzas attributed to Bhasa, though discrepancies put most attributions in doubt. But at least two stanzas are shown as Bhasa's in two anthologies. One describes in a conventional didactic mode the season at the end of the rains:

The sun burns sharply, base but brief,
The deer shed horns, the ungrateful drop friends,
Water pleases, like sages the wise,
And mud starts drying up, like lust in poverty.[6]

The other verse is an unusual variation on a traditional subject:

This mad moonlight turns the whole world's head:
The cat licks it in the cup like milk;
The elephant grasps at its beams through the branches

Mistaking them for tender shoots;
And on the bed it seems a silken sheet
To the maiden at love's end.[7]

But the fame of Bhasa clearly rests at present on his plays.

*

The plays of Bhasa were lost over the course of time. A hundred years ago the text of not a single one of them was available, even though the name of Bhasa had long been esteemed through references in the works of other writers for more than a thousand years. The credit for the rediscovery of his work, it is now accepted, goes to Mahamahopadhyaya T. Ganapati Sastri of Trivandrum. In 1909 this scholar found a palm leaf manuscript containing Sanskrit texts, written in Malayalam characters, of a play evidently composed by Bhasa. The qualification has been added as the author's name did not appear in any of the texts. The authorship had to be inferred from a variety of external and internal evidence. Sastri's researches led to the discovery of other manuscripts, and eventually he recovered thirteen plays which he ascribed to Bhasa and published critically in the Trivandrum Sanskrit Series.[8]

Not unexpectedly, this discovery also resulted in a scholarly controversy about the attribution which has yet to be fully set at rest. This may never happen as the paucity of comprehensive evidence, resulting in different interpretations, remains a feature of ancient Indian historiography. But the prevailing, though not unanimous, scholarly opinion now regards the thirteen plays as the works of Bhasa, and among the earliest examples of Sanskrit drama now available.[9]

Six of these plays are based on the epic *Mahābhārata* story, and presented here in translation. The remaining seven are: *Abhisheka*, *Pratimā*, *Bālacharita*, *Svapna Vāsavadattā*, *Pratijnā Yaugandharāyana*, *Chārudatta* and *Avimāraka*. The plots of the first two of these are drawn from the other Indian epic, the *Rāmāyana*; of the next from the Krishna stories in the *Harivamśa*;

of the next two from the legends about King Udayana; and of the last two from other stories prevalent at the time.

This extant *oeuvre* of Bhasa has been the subject of a certain amount of scholarly research and critical analysis since its discovery.[10] A learned translation into English was made over sixty years ago[11] at the Punjab University. A few of Bhasa's plays have been staged in recent times, both in the original and in translation. But Bhasa's name is still better known than his works, their times, and the contemporary literary and cultural environment. Bhasa himself, the man, is yet to emerge from the shadows of history.

*

The dating of ancient Indian events and figures is rarely an easy process, and often results in numerous theories. It is clear that Bhasa preceded Kalidasa, in whose time the former's plays had already 'established fame'. It has been suggested that Bhasa lived in the Mauryan period, the fourth or the third century BC, as a verse from one of his plays figures in Kautilya's *Arthaśāstra*.[12] But in general, scholarly opinion places him in the first or the second century AD. Ashvaghosha, the biographer of the Buddha and also a noted dramatist, may have lived earlier. But only fragments of one of his plays, the *Sāriputra Prakarana*, have been found in Central Asia. Two satirical monologues by Vararuchi and Isvaradatta are also dated to Bhasa's time or a little earlier. Though this literary form is recognized in classical Indian dramaturgy, it cannot of course be described as a play in the fullest sense. Thus, Bhasa is at present the earliest of the classical Sanskrit dramatists whose plays have come down to us intact.

In historical terms, the time of Bhasa lies between the end of the Mauryan empire and the advent of the Gupta age. It was a period when a number of kingdoms and principalities flourished in India, some of them of considerable size and importance. The Andhra kingdom of the Satavahanas had arisen in the Deccan.

The Kushanas were established in the north-west under the famous Kanishka. The Sakas ruled in the west, and the era named after them, which is still in use, had just commenced. The Cheras controlled the south, and in the east the golden age of Kharavela in Kalinga was a recent memory. In the Gangetic Plain, Bhasa's own reference to the land between the Himalayas and the Vindhyas being under single rule upto the sea, points to the existence of a substantial state.

While this may have been a time of political plurality in the country, it also seems to have been a period of comparative social peace, of increasing economic prosperity and cultural unity, and of wider contacts abroad. Trade had increased, both internally and overseas. Indian merchandise and culture circulated more, not only within the country but also to South-East Asia, the Far East and the Mediterranean. By the middle of the first century Buddhism had reached China, and by the end of that century the Roman Emperor Trajan was receiving an Indian mission in Europe. Internally, mercantile and professional guilds had become wealthy and were providing patronage to learning and the arts. According to a scholarly chronology,[13] the century of Bhasa was also the time of the physician Charaka, the age of the development of Gandhara art, and the period when the Code of Manu assumed its final form.

The cultural achievements mentioned above naturally presuppose a long period of earlier development. The rise of Jainism and Buddhism in India, and subsequently of *bhakti* in its early form, all predate Bhasa by several centuries, not to speak of the much more ancient period of the Vedas and the Upanishads. By the time of Bhasa, Panini's Sanskrit grammar had long been composed, as also Patanjali's famous commentary on it. The Buddhist *Tripitaka* in Pali had also been written. The epic tales of the *Mahābhārata* and the *Rāmāyana* had already become a part of the Indian psyche. The cave temple of Karli and the earlier ones at Ajanta had also been constructed by this period. Nearer the time of Bhasa, Buddhism bifurcated between Mahayana and Hinayana at the great Council summoned by Kanishka. This was also a period of revival of the *sanātana dharma* in India. It is in the background of this rich panorama of past growth and continued creativity of a still vigorous culture that Bhasa's plays were written.

*

The works which have come down to the present from the literature of this period include the Buddha's biography in verse, *Buddhacharita*, and the epic poem *Saundarananda* by Ashvaghosha, the *Rāmāyana*-based play *Kundamālā* by Dinnaga or Dhiranga, and the Buddhist hymns of Matricheta and Nagarjuna, apart from technical treatises like the *Charaka Samhitā* on medicine, and the *Arthaśāstra* on politics. But it is to the Bharata *Nātyaśāstra*[14] that one must turn to acquire a sense of the professional environment in which Bhasa's plays were written and performed. The *Nātyaśāstra* itself is traced to the first or the second century, a period contemporaneous with that of Bhasa. It is the oldest work of Indian fine arts and literary criticism now available, and deals mainly with dramatic representation. It is not a scripture of dance and drama, although it came to be so regarded at a later stage, but rather a compilation of theatrical practices as they had developed over previous centuries, and a theoretical analysis on the basis of these practices. Theories of Sanskrit poetics and literary aesthetics were elaborated further in the works of later critics like Bhamah and Udbhata, Ananda Vardhana, Abhinavagupta and Dhananjaya, between the fifth and tenth centuries. But Bhasa predates them all, and his work, though reflecting to a large extent the canon set down in the *Nātyaśāstra*, follows it less closely than Kalidasa and later dramatists.

The theatre was already a flourishing art form in India in the time of Bhasa and the *Nātyaśāstra*. It had evolved beyond recitals of epic dialogues by hereditary bards. Plays were written and performed often accompanied by music and dance. There were professional producers, actors and actresses, drama teachers and dance instructors. Costumes, make-up, and other aspects of stagecraft were well developed. Performances took place in palaces, in temples and in halls built for the purpose. The *Nātyaśāstra* suggests dimensions of theatre halls for as many as five hundred people, measures for their ventilation, and arrangements for seating the audience. The hall consisted of an auditorium, and a podium with a backstage. In between, a curtain was put up for entries and exits by the players. The similarity between the Sanskrit word for this stage curtain, '*yavanikā*', and for Greek in general '*yavana*', had led some scholars to assume Greek influence on Indian drama in ancient times. But others have concluded that the origin of the two art forms is independent of each other, as their spirits and techniques are quite different. Philologically also, it has been pointed out, that the word for curtain derives from a root pertaining to binding and ropes rather than a Greek connection.[15]

The *Nātyaśāstra* categorizes ten different types of dramatic performances, depending on their theme, length, plot and characters. At one end of this spectrum were the *nātaka* and the *prakarana*, full length plays with five to ten acts, and plots drawn from the epics, history or fiction. At the other end were satirical monologues or *bhanas*. In between there were heroic, tragic or comic plays of one to four acts, and archaic plays about gods and demons. Bhasa's works cover many of these categories. But the translations presented in this collection are, with two exceptions, one-act plays mainly of the types *anka* and *vyāyoga*, evoking respectively the tragic or the heroic flavour.

It would be appropriate at this point to outline briefly the theory of flavour or *rasa* which formed an important and perhaps unique part of ancient Indian poetics. *Rasa* is commonly, but inexactly, also translated as sentiment. Much has been written about it from the classical period onwards. To put it simply, drama is an imitation of life, and specially of emotions, or *bhāva*, which the dramatist shows his characters as experiencing. The audience in turn experiences, not the actual emotion, but an aesthetic appreciation of its *rasa* or flavour. The distinction, apparently subtle, would be clear from the phrase 'to enjoy watching a tragedy'. The skill of the artist lies not only in portraying the emotion on the stage, but also in invoking its flavour in the audience. A cultivated person, able to appreciate a *rasa* with discrimination, was known as a *rasika*.

The *Nātyaśāstra* categorizes eight basic emotions: love (*rati*) humour (*hāsa*), enthusiasm (*utsāha*), anger (*krodha*), fear (*bhaya*), grief (*śoka*), disgust (*jugupsa*), and astonishment (*vismaya*). The corresponding flavours are the erotic (*śringāra*), comic (*hāsya*), heroic (*vīra*), furious (*raudra*), apprehensive (*bhayānaka*), compassionate (*karuna*), horrific (*vībhatsa*), and marvellous (*adbhuta*). At a later time, the emotion of tranquillity and the flavour of calm were added to this list.

Each artistic work was expected to evoke a single predominant flavour. But combinations with other *rasas* were permissible, within certain rules, to enhance the aesthetic effect. Dissection of classical literary works to identify and appraise such combinations was a common activity among scholars and critics. Bhasa combines flavours in his own subtle way. He also evokes new moods, like family affection and comradeship, pride and wilfulness, cunning and guile.

Classical Sanskrit drama had developed certain conventions by the time of Bhasa. Most plays began with a *nāndi* or benediction followed by a prologue, the *prastāvanā* or *sthāpanā*, in which the producer or stage director, called the *sutradhāra*, appeared on the stage with one or more assistants and introduced the play and often the playwright. In most cases the plays also ended with a benediction or *bharata vākya*, generally pronounced by the *sutradhāra*. Between the prologue and the first act, or between the subsequent acts, it was not uncommon to have interludes, called *vishkambhaka* or *praveśaka*, during which the action of the plot was advanced through dialogue between minor characters. Journeys, wars, deaths, and common acts like eating were not represented on the stage, but indicated through such interludes, which even occurred in one-act plays.

The convention about the use of language was that while the more exalted, specially male, characters spoke in classical Sanskrit, the others, and almost all women spoke in the vernacular Prakrit. Scholars believe this to be a reflection of actual life at that time. In later centuries, of course, as Sanskrit became more stylized and artificial, its drama gradually became essentially a court art. But in Bhasa's time it was still an art form with a wider appeal, and his language is comparatively simple and natural.

An important convention, which distinguishes ancient Sanskrit from Greek drama, was the absence in the former of tragic endings and depictions of the hero's death. Several Sanskrit plays have tragic themes or sequences evoking grief, pathos and compassion. But the endings are always auspicious. Learned explanations have been offered for the absence of tragedy in Sanskrit drama, relating it to the philosophy and ethos of India. A straightforward explanation is to be found in a verse from the *Nātyaśāstra* itself: 'Drama is meant for the recreation of the people, of the tired, the miserable, and those in pain and in grief.'[16] Tragic endings could have little place in a recreational activity. From this perspective, as also from that of its descriptions of plot and characterization, it is interesting to reflect upon the extent to which the dicta of the *Nātyaśāstra* can still be traced in that modern form of mass recreation, the Indian cinema.

The construction of a dramatic plot, with its beginning, middle and end, was elaborated in greater detail in the *Nātyaśāstra*. The action of the classic play, passed conventionally through five stages or *avasthā*: start of action; progress; further progress but emergence of difficulties; near-success clouded by obstacles; and final attainment. In a full-length play, each *avasthā* could consist of several dramatic situations showing the characters in action. The story was presented in one or more acts, each encompassing self-contained action within the duration of a day. The acts could be linked by interludes but were not divided into scenes. The plot and characters were drawn mainly from the deeds of legendary or historical heroes, but they also dealt with contemporary life, both élite and ordinary. According to the *Nātyaśāstra*, both the hero and plot should be well-known. Nobility and self-possession were the expected traits of all types of heroes who were otherwise categorized as calm, gay, proud or magnanimous. The categorization of heroines was much more elaborate: maidenly or mature; with or without a husband; awaiting the lover or going for a tryst. There were at least eight types of heroines in literature with many permutations and sub-divisions. The supporting cast included villains, jesters, companions and other stock characters. An important character was the *sutradhāra*, literally the string-holder, like a puppeteer, who introduced the play as its producer and director, and occasionally acted as standby in other roles. In the prologue of one of the plays included in this collection, *Dūta Ghatotkacham*, Bhasa describes the cosmic drama of the universe, directed from its beginning to the final curtain, by a divine *sutradhāra*.

The Sanskrit play had short but clear stage directions for all actions from entry to exit. Action proceeded through dialogue, asides, soliloquy and imaginary dialogue. It seems there were not many stage props or accessories. In most cases they were evoked through dialogue and gestures. Song and dance were often included. This was the theatrical craft of Bhasa's days.

*

As already mentioned, Bhasa's work is marked by some interesting departures from the conventions described in the *Nātyaśāstra*. First, he dispenses with the opening benediction or *nāndi*. None of the plays in the present collection have this exordium, but begin in each case with the stage direction, 'after the *nāndi*, enter the *sutradhāra*'. This distinctive feature was remarked upon as long ago as the time of Bana Bhatta who had noted that Bhasa's producer does pronounce a benediction in his own first words. Interestingly, his subsequent remarks are more or less identical in all these plays.

The closing benediction is also absent in some of the plays in this collection. The five stages of dramatic development are difficult to trace in most cases, but this may be due to the compactness of the plots and the pace of action in the one-act plays. But Bhasa's most noteworthy breach of convention lies in giving a tragic ending in one play with the hero's death on stage.

The play *Urubhangam* ends with the death of the hero, Duryodhana, who has earlier been vanquished in battle and humiliated. It is a powerful tragedy in modern terms, and perhaps explicable conventionally only if the hero's end is regarded as his ascent to heaven. Three other plays, *Dūta Vākyam*, *Dūta Ghatotkacham* and *Karnabhāram* have strong evocations of oncoming tragedy and doom, though they do not actually end with death. In all four, Bhasa has devised a form of dramatic presentation of which there are no other examples in classical Sanskrit literature.

Bhasa's characterizations are in keeping with convention. The most interesting character in his plays, based on the *Mahābhārata*, is without doubt Duryodhana. This principal villain of the actual epic is presented in four of these plays as the *dhīroddhata* type of hero, proud and haughty, wilful and defiant, but withal noble and self-possessed. Courage, magnanimity and piety are other qualities with which Bhasa invests Duryodhana who is also shown as a devoted son, a loving father, a good friend and a man both royal and loyal. Other characters brought to life in the plays are Duryodhana's father, the old blind king Dhritarashtra, his cunning uncle, Shakuni, and his chief adversaries, the three Pandava princes. His friend Karna is the noble, tragic hero of the play *Karnabhāram*. His protagonist in another play, *Dūta Vākyam*, is Krishna, depicted with an enigmatic mix of both human and divine attributes. But the sense of Krishna's divinity is present in the other plays also.

In view of the deity invoked at the beginning of his plays it has been suggested that Bhasa was a devotee of the god Vishnu, and a follower of the Bhagavata cult.[17] The opening lines of the plays in the present collection address Vishnu by some of his well-known traditional appellations like Narayana, Hari, Sridhara, Upendra and Kesava. The last is clearly identified with Krishna. The doctrine of the incarnations of Vishnu seems to have been well-established by Bhasa's time. Apart from Rama and Krishna, there is mention in Bhasa's invocations of Narasimha, the god's incarnation as man-lion, and of the three strides with which the dwarf incarnation, Vamana, bestrode the universe. The plays depict a time of orthodox religious rituals and practices like fire sacrifices and the ceremonial use of water in making vows and incantations. The society portrayed in them already had the main elements of the caste hierarchy. The principal characters in Bhasa's plays, based on the *Mahābhārata*, are drawn almost entirely from the priestly and the warrior castes. The former expected and received respect and regard from the others. The warrior caste had a recognized code of chivalry and honour. But Bhasa's characters are not caste stereotypes. Their individuality and human reality is apparent even in minor characters like soldiers, chamberlains and cowherds.

*

Before considering the plays based on the *Mahābhārata* which are featured in the present collection, a brief reference to the other seven plays of Bhasa would be in order.[18] The most acclaimed of these is *Svapna Vāsavadattā*, in six acts, based on the legend of the gallant king Udayana, his wives the beloved Vasavadatta and the beautiful Padmavati, and his wise and loyal minister, Yaugandharayana. The play derives its name from a central episode in which the king dreams of the queen he thinks is dead. Its companion play *Pratijnā Yaugandharāyana* tells the earlier story of the king's romance with Vasavadatta. Udayana is a historical figure and a contemporary of the Buddha. There are many legends about his adventures.

Chārudatta is named after the hero with whom the courtesan Vasantasena falls in love. The story, with its supporting cast of scoundrels and jesters, is refashioned and continued in the better known *Mrichhakatika* of Sudraka written a century later. It is a story based on fiction, as is that of *Avimāraka*, another six-act play about mistaken identity and magic. The final benedictory verse is the same as in *Pratijnā*.

The two plays drawn from the *Rāmāyana, Pratimā* and *Abhisheka*, are long, seven and six acts respectively, and deal with Rama's exile in the forest, the abduction and rescue of his wife, and his eventual return to his capital. The first derives its name from an episode involving the statue of the hero's father, and the second from his own final consecration, and that of his ally, the monkey-king, Sugriva, with which the play begins. In both, the playwright includes some episodes not to be found in the original epic.

An important difference is that in the first play Rama has a human characterization, while in the second he is definitely identified with the god Vishnu. The second play also depicts death on stage, the killing of the monkey-king's brother by Rama. This unconventional feature is also present in *Bālacharita*, which describes the adventures of Krishna as a boy, culminating in his slaying of the villain-king Kamsa. The epilogue of this play is identical with that of *Svapna Vāsavadattā* and *Dūta Vākyam*, referring to a vast kingdom in the Gangetic Plain.

The six *Mahābhārata* plays have certain common characteristics which give them a measure of unity, and set them apart as a group by itself. To begin with, they are inspired by the same great epic and the same epic characters appear or are mentioned in all of them. Something of the ruggedness of that tale of war also seems to have permeated these plays. The gay and delicate erotic flavour, so beloved of Sanskrit dramatists, is totally absent in them. But their most interesting feature is perhaps their nearness to the modern idiom. They are comparatively short and fast paced. The drama unfolds rapidly, the dialogue is often terse. The literary embellishments, so profuse in later classical authors, are used with relative restraint. The evocation of impending doom also has a modern ring. To vivify his characters and obtain dramatic effects, Bhasa often departs from the epic into episodes of his own creation. One play, *Pancharātram*, indeed ends with an imminent peace between the warring sides.

Each play is built around a particular point or sequence in the narrative of the epic story, as it moves inexorably from dispute to war to destruction. In terms of this movement, the first play is *Madhyama Vyāyoga* in which the Pandava princes, the heroes of the epic, are in enforced exile following the machinations of their cousins and enemies, the Kauravas. Then comes *Pancharātram*, in which the exile draws to an end and tensions seem to subside. It is followed by *Dūta Vākyam* in which a peaceful solution is attempted, but fails. In the next play, *Dūta Ghatotkacham*, the war has already commenced, and now passes the point of no return. There follows *Karnabhāram*, with premonitions of the defeat of the Kauravas. The final battle takes place in *Urubhangam*, with the death of the Kaurava leader.

To place these plays in their complete perspective, it is useful to have an overview of the epic's main narrative as a whole. The *Mahābhārta* plays were, of course, written for audiences fully familiar with the stories of the epic and with the main characters participating in them. Without this familiarity it is not possible to understand all the references or to savour the *rasa* in full, even though there are dramatic scenes which stand on their own. Many readers would already be familiar in greater or lesser detail with the *Mahābhārata* which has, in recent years, reached a larger and more international audience through the media of television, film and theatre. The following paragraphs are, as such, intended mainly for other readers who do not have this familiarity. The very brief summary contained in them gives essentially the background of the six plays under consideration here.[19]

*

One may begin with the common ancestor of the warring sides, Vichitravirya of the Kuru dynasty. He was the king of Hastinapura, which is near Delhi, the present capital of India. This personage became king, as his elder half-brother, the noble Bhishma, had renounced the throne and taken a vow of life-long celibacy for reasons which are another story in the epic. Vichitravirya died while still young, and the sons of his two wives were brought up under Bhishma's care. As the elder boy, Dhritarashtra, was blind from birth, his younger half-brother, Pandu was consecrated king in due course. Then Pandu died and Dhritarashtra became the king.

Pandu had five sons who bore the patronymic Pandava. Dhritarashtra had one hundred sons who were known by the dynastic name Kaurava. The eldest of the one-hundred-and-five cousins was Pandu's firstborn, Yudhishthira. However, his right to the throne was contested by Dhritarashtra's eldest son, Duryodhana.

As the main narrative commences, a blind king is on the throne while his sons and nephews, now on the threshold of manhood, dispute the succession. The kingdom is guarded by the now venerable Bhishma who has engaged a famous teacher, Drona, for his grand-nephews. The Pandava princes are brilliant: Yudhisthira in wisdom, Bhima in strength, Arjuna in archery. The Kauravas are envious. But Duryodhana wins the friendship of Karna, a superb warrior of apparently humble origin but, unknown to himself and to everyone else, the illegitimate son of Pandu's wife, Kunti, and so the eldest brother of the Pandavas.

A conspiracy by Duryodhana to have them murdered forces the Pandavas to flee and eventually take refuge in the neighbouring kingdom of Panchala. There, in the sole instance of polyandry in the epic, they all marry Draupadi, the daughter of the local king. Fortified with this alliance, they return to Hastinapura. In a compromise, a portion of the ancestral kingdom is set aside for them and Yudhishthira becomes an independent king. His new kingdom prospers and is further strengthened by another matrimonial alliance, between the third Pandava prince Arjuna, and the sister of the Yadava chief Krishna who is also a cousin from their mother's side. Yudhishthira performs a royal sacrificial ceremony and assumes imperial prerogatives. He is universally acclaimed as a righteous ruler.

The Kauravas had also attended the Pandava sacrifice, to which they had been invited despite past enemity. The magnificence of the ceremony and the splendour of the Pandava court filled them with envy and made them feel belittled. To hurt pride was added rage, when on this occasion Draupadi ridiculed and insulted Duryodhana who had also been an aspirant for her hand at one time. He and his brothers returned to Hastinapura, determined to settle scores with the Pandavas in some way.

Duryodhana had an evil genius in his maternal uncle Shakuni who was also an expert gamesman with dice. With his encouragement, King Yudhishthira was invited to Hastinapura for a gambling match, an invitation he could not refuse both because of the requirements of the code of chivalry, and his own weakness for the game of dice. At the game Shakuni, playing on behalf of his nephew, cheated and won. Yudhishthira staked in turn, his wealth, his kingdom, his brothers, and then himself, but lost them all, in throw after throw.

Finally, Yudhishthira was induced to stake the Pandavas' common queen Draupadi, and lost her too. As the Pandavas watched in shame and anger, she was dragged into the gaming hall on Duryodhana's orders. There she was publicly humiliated. Karna called her a harlot. Duryodhana bared his thigh and beckoned her to sit on it. His brother attempted to strip her naked. Draupadi reacted with great spirit, questioning her husband's right to stake her when he had already lost himself and was no longer a free agent, and appealing to the shocked Kaurava elders. Sensing that the match had gone too far, the blind king ordered a replay, with the wager that the losing side would go into exile for twelve years, followed by one year's exile in hiding when, should they be discovered, the twelve years would be repeated again. Shakuni won this last stake also, and the Pandavas were forced into exile.

The Kauravas attempted to harass the Pandavas in this trying time, but were ignominiously rebuffed. The Pandavas had many adventures during their exile. Arjuna succeeded in his search for celestial weapons which made him invincible. Eventually the twelve years drew to an end and the Pandavas prepared to go into hiding for the final phase of the exile.

They disguised themselves and entered the service of King Virata. Yudhishthira became the king's companion and gaming partner. Bhima became the royal cook. Arjuna, masquerading as a eunuch, became the dance instructor of the king's daughter. The two younger Pandavas were appointed respectively as a groom and a cowherd. Draupadi was employed as the maid of Virata's queen. But their troubles had not yet ended. The queen's powerful brother became infatuated with Draupadi. His overtures became so excessive that Bhima was secretly obliged to murder him and his associates. The news of this event spread far. It reached the Kauravas who had been searching for their hidden adversaries, and they suspected it may lead them to a discovery. Consequently they mounted a probing expedition against King Virata, ostensibly to seize his cattle.

When the news of this attack reached Virata's capital, he and his army were engaged on another frontier of the kingdom and only his young son was at home. Draupadi persuaded this prince to go forth against the invaders with Arjuna, in his eunuch's garb as the charioteer. The latter took charge of the battle and routed the Kauravas. It then became obvious that the Pandavas had been discovered. But the year of hiding had also ended coincidentally at the same time. The Pandavas proclaimed their identity. Virata's daughter was married to Arjuna's son in another dynastic alliance. This young warrior was also the nephew of Krishna, the Yadava chief who had emerged as a close friend and adviser of the Pandavas.

The Pandavas now looked to regaining their kingdom. They also thirsted to avenge the dishonour and deprivation they had suffered at Kaurava hands. Only Yudhishthira, ever the righteous ruler, sought to avoid war. It was eventually decided that Krishna should go to the Kaurava court to seek a peaceful solution. However, Krishna's mission failed: the Pandavas were prepared to settle for the return of only five villages; but Duryodhana, defiantly insisting that their claims were spurious, refused to part with even a needle point of land. The blind king could do nothing because of his love for his son. Bhishma, Drona and the other Kuru elders acknowledged the justice of the Pandava claim, but felt bound by their loyalty to the throne of Hastinapura. War became inevitable.

Both sides gathered enormous armies. Practically all the chiefs of the time joined one camp or the other. Krishna's brother Balarama alone refused to take sides. Krishna himself agreed to become Arjun's charioteer in battle, while he sent his army to fight for the Kauravas. Other notable Kaurava supporters, apart from Karna and Shakuni, were Duryodhana's brother-in-law Jayadratha, King of Sindhu, and King Shalya, the maternal uncle of the two younger Pandavas, who was tricked by Duryodhana into joining him. The Pandava allies included King Virata and the father of Draupadi, as also the ogre Ghatokacha, the son of Bhima by a demon-princess, conceived during their first flight from Hastinapura.

The war took place on the plains of Kurukshetra. At the moment of its commencement, when Arjuna saw all the relatives and friends arrayed against each other in the opposing armies, he was so depressed that he laid down his weapons and declared that the bloodshed was pointless. But Krishna manifested his divine aspect and, in the famous discourse of the Bhagavad Gita, exhorted Arjuna to do his duty in what was a conflict between right and wrong.

The fighting lasted eighteen days. There were many feats of valour and guile, generosity and brutality. At first, while the noble patriarch Bhishma commanded the Kaurava armies, the code of chivalry and the rules of warfare were respected. But gradually they were broken by both sides. Knowing that Bhishma would not bear arms against a eunuch, the Pandavas cunningly sent one against him, and Arjuna shot the old general down from behind. Then Arjuna's young son, Abhimanyu, was lured into unequal combat and killed by the Kauravas. Drona, who had taught the martial arts to the princes on both sides, was in turn killed when he had stopped fighting as a result of false information confirmed to him by none other than the righteous Yudhishthira. Each such incident inflamed passions and made certain that the war would continue.

From the Kaurava side Karna alone was considered a match for Arjuna. Just before the war he had been told by Krishna, and by his natural mother, about his relationship with the Pandavas and invited to change sides. But he refused to do so, remaining steadfastly loyal to his friend Duryodhana. Thereafter he was tricked into parting with his magic armour and exhausting his most potent weapon before he had the opportunity of facing Arjuna. He went into that combat with a premonition that he would die. It was a marvellous duel, watched by the gods. Eventually Arjuna was able to kill him, unchivalrously, while he was trying to pull out his chariot wheel stuck in the ground.

Ultimately, the Kaurava side was almost entirely destroyed. Only Duryodhana and a few others remained. Wounded and tired, Duryodhana hid in a lake where he was found by the Pandavas. He challenged them to single combat, and a great duel with maces then took place between him and Bhima. Finally, Bhima brought him down with a foul blow which shattered his thigh, the same thigh that he had bared for Draupadi. Vanquished but still defiant, Duryodhana berated Krishna and the Pandavas for their perfidies and boasted that while they suffered a war-ravaged world, he would have an honoured place in heaven befitting a true warrior and king.

As Duryodhana lay dying, he appointed Drona's son as his new commander and approved his plans for a midnight massacre of the Pandava forces. This scheme was carried out and only the five brothers escaped. Thereafter Yudhishthira ruled justly for many years. But joy had gone out of the times with the destruction of war. Eventually Yudhishthira departed with his wife and brothers to seek salvation in the high Himalayas, leaving the kingdom to Arjuna's grandson.

*

By the time of Bhasa the epic story had been told and retold over the centuries, and its principal characters and their deeds had already made a deep impact on popular imagination. First, there were the five Pandava brothers with their exemplary loyalty and devotion to each other. Pandu was their father only in name: actually they had been begotten of the gods. Endowed with qualities of semi-divine excellence, they were nevertheless intensely human. Yudhishthira was virtue and wisdom incarnate, but still prone to human errors and lapses which he later regretted bitterly. Bhima was simple but stronger than ten thousand elephants and swift as the wind; he was also given to gluttony and moved by violent passions. Arjuna, a romantic knight, was the warrior without equal. His son Abhimanyu, the beloved of the whole family, showed promise of excelling his father, but was killed before reaching his prime. The other two Pandava brothers, the twins, Nakula and Sahadeva, were noted for their comeliness and learning. The queen Draupadi was beautiful, imperious and the moving spirit in keeping steeled the resolve of her five husbands to avenge the wrongs they had suffered.

The Kauravas were less virtuous, but not without nobility. Duryodhana's envy and jealousy of his cousins had gradually turned into an obsession. But he was proud, courageous and kingly. His uncle Shakuni incited him to wickedness, but was personally brave and devoted to him. His friend, the noble warrior Karna, was loyal and generous to a fault. His father, blind in life, was also blind to his shortcomings because he loved him too deeply. His grand-uncle Bhishma and his preceptor Drona, respected elders of the kingdom, tried their best to bring the two sides together. Bhasa highlights the noble qualities of all these characters in his plays.

Krishna has an ambivalent role in the epic, both human and divine. As an incarnation he upholds virtue, suppresses wickedness and shows the path to salvation. At a human level his advice is often worldly and amoral. Bhasa reflects both these aspects in his characterization.

*

Finally, a few words about these translations. It is well known that because of differences in linguistic construction and literary convention, literal or even too faithful translations from Sanskrit into English often become unreadable. To attempt to bridge the distance between the letter and the spirit of one language and that of the other is the real challenge for any translator. As indicated at the beginning of this note, a scholarly translation of these plays already exists. The endeavour in the present instance has been to produce not a work for scholars but rather a translation into readable English which can also convey something of the pace and flavour of the original plays. In the process, a few abridgements have been made without which, in the translator's opinion, the English version would have tended to drag. In the same context the system of diacritics has largely been dispensed with in the transliteration of names, and more commonplace spellings adopted.

I have worked from the Sanskrit text published in 1967 in Varanasi by Chowkhamba Vidyabhawan with the commentaries of Ramji Mishra. The latter have been a valuable aid in my work. These translations first appeared in the Sunday editions of the *National Herald* of New Delhi, and I am grateful to A.N. Dar, then Editor-in-Chief of that newspaper, for agreeing to their publication in book form. I am also grateful to M.L. Nankani for preparing the typescripts and to Madhav K. Dar for reading and commenting on most of them in the first instance. I further thank P.K. Arora for typing the introduction and the notes.

Belgrade A.N.D.H.
June 1991

The Middle One

Madhyama Vyāyoga

{1}

The Middle One

Madhyama Vyāyoga

The original title of this play is derived from two of its main characters, and from the type of the dramatic composition. In classical Sanskrit dramaturgy the *vyāyoga* was a one-act play evoking the heroic mood, devoid of any romantic element, and with few feminine roles among its other specified characteristics. The present play comes within this categorization.

The word *madhyama* here refers to the middle one among three brothers. It was not uncommon for the middle brother to be called as such. Even today, the derivative word *manjhalā* is used in common parlance in parts of North India in referring to the middle brother. Two of the characters in this play, the son of the priest Keshava Dasa and the Pandava prince, Bhimasena, are addressed as *madhyama*; and the dramatic plot is advanced by the confusion thus caused. This is a central feature of the play and explains its title.

Bhima of course was the second of the five Pandava brothers. But he was the middle one of the three sons born to the queen Kunti. These three, Yudhishthira, Bhima and Arjuna, are among the leading characters of the *Mahābhārata*. Bhima was begotten of the god of wind, and was renowned for his strength and swiftness. The other two Pandavas were the twins, Nakula and Sahdeva, who were the sons of the queen Madri. They are figures of lesser importance in the epic.

The other main character in this play is the ogre Ghatotkacha, the son of Bhima and Hidimba. The story in the epic goes that when the Pandava brothers were fleeing through a forest following a conspiracy by their cousins, the Kauravas, to murder them, they were chanced upon by an ogre who sent his sister Hidimba to entice them. She fell in love with Bhima who was keeping watch. Bhima later killed the ogre and married Hidimba. After the birth of their son, Hidimba agreed to leave Bhima who continued with his brothers in further adventures. Ghatotkacha does not reappear in the epic till the war between the Pandavas and Kauravas begins. Then he comes in support of his father and uncles, and eventually dies in battle against the Kaurava warrior Karna.

There is no other mention of Ghatotkacha in the *Mahābhārata*. The story of the present play is evidently Bhasa's own creation. It is set in the time when the Pandavas were in exile after their kingdom had been lost to the Kauravas in the famous game of dice. But the episode of the priest Keshava Dasa and his sons, and the subsequent encounter and battle between Ghatotkacha and Bhima in the forest do not exist in the epic.

The theme of an encounter between father and son, in which neither recognizes the other, and sometimes fight each other, is not unknown in other literature. Bhasa makes full use of it in this play to create a dramatic effect and to evoke a sense of familial affection as well as the heroic mood. At the same time his invention of the Keshava Dasa family and its poignant dilemma provides a contrast between the epic figures and the more down-to-earth characters in the play.

Both the opening benediction and the epilogue of this play invoke the god Vishnu through his synonyms Hari and Upendra. To facilitate understanding, only the former name has been used in the present translation. The opening verse refers to Vishnu's incarnation as a dwarf. According to the myth this incarnation appeared before the demon-king Bali, the power of whose piety and virtues was threatening to dethrone the gods from paradise and make him the ruler of the universe. In the guise of a supplicant, the divine dwarf requested the king for three strides worth of land, to which the latter agreed. Then, with his first cosmic stride the dwarf bestrode the earth and with his second the heavens. His kingdom gone, the virtuous king offered his own head for the placing of the third step, and was blessed for his devotion. The three strides were a popular theme in artistic representations. A fine example is the rock-cut relief at Mamallapuram near Madras and another at Badami in the state of Karnataka.

The play is indicative of the respect in which the priestly caste was held by others. In this it also provides a social comment on the time.

Cast in order of appearance

The Producer	*in the Prologue*
A Priest	*named Keshava Dasa*
First	*his eldest son*
Second	*his middle son*
Third	*his youngest son*
The Wife	*of the priest*
Ghatotkacha	*son of Bhimasena and Hidimba*
Bhimasena	*the middle Pandava prince*
Hidimba	*a demon princess*

Prologue

[After the benediction, enter the Producer]

PRODUCER The foot of Hari is pure as the lotus and blue as the blade of a sword. Upraised to straddle the three worlds, it shines against the sky like a bridge of sapphires across the sea, even as the hearts of demon princesses sink. May that foot protect you all.

And now, distinguished spectators, I have to announce that—but what is that? There seems to be a sound just as I was about to start. Well, let me see.

[Voice off stage]

VOICE O father, who is this?

PRODUCER Ah, I see. From the accent and the tone it is clear that a priest is being harassed by some brazen villain.

[Voice off stage]

VOICE O father, who is this?

PRODUCER Oh, it is very clear. The son of the middle Pandava, born of the demoness Hidimba, is harassing some innocent priests. Alas, here is this aged priest with his wife, surrounded by their young and frightened sons. They are being followed by that ogre, and are desperate like a bull with his cow and scared little calves in terror of a stalking tiger.

[Exit]

[END OF PROLOGUE]

ACT I

[Enter an old priest with his three sons and wife, followed by Ghatotkacha]

PRIEST O who is this? His hair shines like the rays of the morning sun. His eyes are amber under a knotted brow. The chain around his neck flashes like lightning. He looks like the day of judgement.

FIRST O father, who is this? His hair is yellow like gold. His eyes are like two planets. His chest is vast and covered with yellow silk. His colour is concentrated darkness and his white teeth stick out like the crescent moon from the clouds.

SECOND Who is this, dark like a cloud? His teeth are like the tusks of a baby elephant. His nose is as a plough. His arms are like elephant trunks. His wrath blazes like a sacrificial fire.

THIRD O father, who is this terrorizing us, like a lion with a herd of deer or a falcon with a flock of birds. He is like a thunderbolt striking a mountain peak, like death personified.

WIFE Sir, who is this, persecuting us?

GHATOTKACHA Wait, O priest, wait. I have scared all courage out of you. You are unable to protect your frightened wife and children. You are like a snake before an angry eagle. Where are you going? Stop, priest, stop.

PRIEST Do not be afraid, wife. Children, do not be afraid. He speaks with discrimination.

GHATOTKACHA Alas! I know very well that noble priests should always be revered everywhere on this earth. Yet, my mother's command must be carried out and I must do today what should never be done.

PRIEST Wife, don't you remember that holy sage saying that this forest is inhabited by ogres and one must travel carefully. Even so this horror has come our way.

WIFE Why do you look so resigned, sir?

PRIEST What can I do? It is my misfortune.

WIFE Let us shout for help.

FIRST Mother, whom shall we shout for? This dark forest is inhabited only by animals. It is deserted and fit only for hermits.

PRIEST Do not be afraid, wife. I am relieved to hear that it is fit for hermits. I think that the Pandava hermitage cannot be far from here. The Pandavas are brave warriors. They help the poor and protect the helpless. They will be able to punish such wicked people suitably.

FIRST Father, I don't think the Pandavas are there.

PRIEST How do you know?

FIRST I heard from a priest who had come from there that they have gone to attend a sacrifice at the hermitage of the sage Dhaumya.

PRIEST Then we are dead!

FIRST But not all of them, father. I believe the middle one has stayed behind to guard their hermitage.

PRIEST He is equal to all the Pandavas put together.

FIRST But I heard that at this time he goes to some other place for his sport.

PRIEST Then there is no hope. Very well, son, let me entreat this one.

FIRST It is useless.

PRIEST Son, we will beseech him to let us go. Let us see. Sir, is it possible to let us go?

GHATOTKACHA It is possible on one condition.

PRIEST And what is the condition?

GHATOTKACHA There is my lady mother. She commanded me, 'Son, find me some human in this forest for breaking my fast.' So, I have caught you. If you would like me to release you and your good wife and two of your sons, then make a selection and leave one son to me.

PRIEST You wicked ogre! Am I not a priest? I am an old and learned priest. How could I be happy abandoning a well-brought-up son to a man-eating ogre?

GHATOTKACHA Then, O best among priests, if you will not leave one son to me as I have requested, you and your whole family will perish in a moment.

PRIEST Then this is my decision. This old and well-used body of mine has done all it had to do. To preserve my sons I offer it to the fire which is this ogre.

WIFE No, no, sir. The husband is everything for a devoted wife. This body has served its purpose. I will give it to protect you and the family.

GHATOTKACHA No, madam. My mother does not want a woman.

PRIEST I will go with you, sir.

GHATOTKACHA Stand aside, old man.

FIRST Father, may I say something?

PRIEST Say it quickly.

FIRST I wish to give my life in exchange for yours. Please let me go for the sake of this family.

SECOND No, noble one. The eldest is the first in the family, and the most important. He is the dearest to the parents. In keeping with the traditions of our elders, it is I who will go.

FIRST No, my dear. If the father is in difficulty, it is for the eldest son to relieve him. Therefore, I will go to save our father's life.

PRIEST The eldest is the dearest to me. I cannot bear to let him go.

WIFE Sir, just as the eldest is dear to you, so is the youngest to me.

SECOND The least dear to parents! Now whom can he please.

GHATOTKACHA I am pleased. Come quickly.

SECOND I am fortunate that my life will be used to save the lives of my elders. Love for one's body is nothing compared to the love for the family.

GHATOTKACHA How wonderful is the devotion of this priest's son to his family.

SECOND Father, I salute you.

PRIEST My devoted son! In exchanging your own life for that of your father, may you attain the highest heaven.

SECOND I am grateful. Mother, I salute you.

WIFE May you live long, son.

SECOND I am grateful. Sir, I salute you.

FIRST My dear, embrace me deeply, even as all the virtues embrace you. And your fame will be embraced by this earth.

SECOND I am grateful.

THIRD Sir, I salute you.

SECOND Good luck.

THIRD I am grateful.

SECOND Sir, I want to say something.

GHATOTKACHA Say it quickly.

SECOND I see a lake in this forest. Now that I am pledged for the next world, I would first like to quench my thirst.

GHATOTKACHA Go, resolute one. But my mother's dinner time is passing. So come back quickly.

SECOND O father, I go. (*Exit*).

PRIEST Alas! We have been robbed. We have been robbed. My sons were like a mountain with three peaks. Now the middle peak is shattered and I am sick at heart. O my boy, how have you gone! You were young and fair, disciplined and brilliant. Now you go to your destruction, like a tree in bloom uprooted by an elephant.

GHATOTKACHA The priest's son is late. My mother's dinner time is passing. What should I do? I see. O priest, call your son.

PRIEST Ah! your words are most cruel.

GHATOTKACHA Why are you getting angry? Bear with me, sir, bear with me. This is my nature. Well, what is your son called?

PRIEST I am unable to bear even these words.

GHATOTKACHA Very well. O priest's son, what is your brother's name?

FIRST Poor middle one.

GHATOTKACHA Middle one? It is a very appropriate name. I will call him. Middle one, O middle one, come quickly.

[Enter Bhimasena]

BHIMA Whose voice is that? Who calls out in this dense forest full of chirping birds. That voice is very similar to Arjuna's and fills me with curiosity.

GHATOTKACHA The priest's son is very late. My mother's dinner time is passing. What shall I do? Well, I see. I will call out loudly. O middle one, come quickly.

BHIMA O who calls me middle one in this forest and disturbs my sport. Let me see. (*Walks around and looks with wonder*) O what a handsome person! He is like a lion, with pale eyes and brows, shining mane and a deep and smooth throat. His chest is broad, his middle taut and his arms and shoulders are strong like those of a bull or an elephant. His nose is aquiline. Clearly he is the son of some powerful warrior from a demoness.

GHATOTKACHA The priest's son is late. I will call out loudly. Ho, middle one, come quickly.

BHIMA Ho, here I am.

GHATOTKACHA He is not the priest's son. O, but what a handsome person! He is like a lion. His arms are golden columns, his shoulders bright as the eagle's wing. His waist is small and his eyes are large like blooming lotuses. Is he the god Vishnu? He attracts me like a kinsman just arrived. O middle one, I have been calling you.

BHIMA So, I am here.

GHATOTKACHA Sir, are you also the middle one?

BHIMA Without doubt, my good sir. I am the middle one among the invincible exiled brothers.

GHATOTKACHA You are?

BHIMA Also, I am the middle one—the wind—among the five elements and among the kings. In fact I am the middle one in all things.

PRIEST His words are such that he is obviously the middle Pandava, come here to release us from the terror of death.

[Enter the Second brother]

SECOND I have drunk the bright water of that lotus-filled lake. I have offered water for my own funeral. (*Approaching*) Sir, here I am.

GHATOTKACHA You, sir, are the real middle one. Come this way.

PRIEST (*Approaching Bhima*) O middle one, save this priest's family.

BHIMA Do not be afraid. Do not be afraid. The middle one salutes you.

PRIEST May you be long-lived like the wind.

BHIMA Thank you. Of what is the noble one afraid?

PRIEST Please listen. I am Keshava Dasa from the Mathara clan. I am the priest of Yupa village in Kurukshetra which was formerly ruled by King Yudhishthira. My uncle Yagya Datta lives in Udyamaka village in the north. I was going to his son's sacred thread ceremony with my spouse.

BHIMA May you have a safe journey. And then?

PRIEST And then this ogre in front of you, dark as a cloud and fearsome as a lion, wishes to kill me with my wife and children.

BHIMA I see. He has obstructed the priest's journey. Well, I will deal with him. Wait, sir!

GHATOTKACHA I am here.

BHIMA Why are you troubling this priestly family? This old priest is like the moon with sons like stars, and you are trying to eclipse him?

GHATOTKACHA What else?

BHIMA Let this harmless priest go with his wife and sons. Priests are not killed even if they have committed crimes.

GHATOTKACHA I will not let him go.

BHIMA (*Aside*) O whose son is this? He has the qualities of all my brothers. Seeing his youthful pride I am reminded of the son of Subhadra. (*Aloud*) Let them go, sir!

GHATOTKACHA I won't. Even if my father were to ask me emphatically to release them, I will not do so, because I have taken them at my mother's command.

BHIMA (*Aside*) Mother's command? This poor fellow is indeed devoted to his mother. Well, for a man the mother is indeed the god of gods. We ourselves are in this condition, having honoured our mother's instruction. (*Aloud*) I want to ask you something.

GHATOTKACHA Do it quickly.

BHIMA Who is your mother, sir?

GHATOTKACHA She is the demoness named Hidimba. She was espoused by the high-souled Pandava as the sky is by the full moon.

BHIMA (*Aside, happily*) So, this is Hidimba's son! His pride is appropriate. He is like his parents in beauty, prowess and capability. But from where has he got a temperament devoid of compassion for the people. (*Aloud*) Let them go!

GHATOTKACHA I will not.

BHIMA Take your son, O priest, I will go with this one.

SECOND No, no, sir. I have already decided to give up my life for that of my parents. You are virtuous, handsome and in your prime. Your place is on this earth.

BHIMA No, sir. I am born in a family of warriors. Priests are to be revered. That is why I wish to exchange my body for that of the priest.

GHATOTKACHA So, he is a warrior. That is why he is proud. Well I will kill him and take the other. Who will stop me?

BHIMA I will.

GHATOTKACHA What? You!

BHIMA Who else.

GHATOTKACHA In that case you had better come with me.

BHIMA I follow the strongest. If you have strength, take me by force.

GHATOTKACHA Do you know who I am, sir?

BHIMA I know you as my son.

GHATOTKACHA What? How am I your son?

BHIMA Do not get angry. Forgive me, sir. Warriors address all the populace with the term 'son'. Therefore I addressed you in the same way.

GHATOTKACHA You are using the language of cowards.

BHIMA I swear I do not know what fear is. In fact I have come to learn what it is, sir. You appear to be an expert on the subject. So tell me what it is like.

GHATOTKACHA I will instruct you in fear. Take up your weapons.

BHIMA I hold my weapon.

GHATOTKACHA What do you mean?

BHIMA Here is my natural weapon, my right arm. It is like a column of gold. I use it to put down my foes.

GHATOTKACHA Only my father Bhimasena has the right to use such language.

BHIMA And who is this Bhima? The god of creation, the god of destruction, the king of heaven, the powerful god of death—does your father compare with any of these, sir?

GHATOTKACHA With all of them.

BHIMA Shame on you! That is a lie!

GHATOTKACHA A lie! You belittle my father? I will uproot this tree and strike him. (*Strikes*) What, it has no effect? Well, what should I do now? I see. I will uproot this mountain peak and strike him with it. This will certainly kill him.

BHIMA The wild elephant, even if angry, does not engage a tiger in the forest.

GHATOTKACHA (*Striking*) What, even this has no effect. What should I do now? I see. Stand still! I am the son of Bhimasena and the grandson of the wind god. There is none as well prepared as I in wrestling.

[Both wrestle]

GHATOTKACHA (*Putting Bhima in a lock*) You cannot escape from my strong arms. You are tied down like an elephant with strong ropes.

BHIMA (*Aside*) How has he caught me? Protect yourself, O Duryodhana, your enemies are getting stronger. (*Aloud*) On guard, sir!

GHATOTKACHA I am ready.

BHIMA (*Breaking lock*) Do not be too proud of your strength, warrior. I have seen it. Wrestling with you does not trouble me at all.

GHATOTKACHA Even this had no effect! What should I do now? I see. There is the magic noose given by mother. I will tie him in that and take him. Now, where is some water? O mountain, some water. Ah, it flows. (*Sips and makes an incantation*) Well, man, bound in the magic noose you will be like the ceremonial flagstaff at a festival, tied with ropes. You will be forced to follow me. (*Ties him*)

BHIMA What? I am bound in the magic noose? What will I do now? I see. There is the antidote to magic nooses which the great god gave me. I will use that incantation. Where is some water? O son of the priest, bring me some water from your container.

PRIEST Here is the water.

[Bhima sips, makes an incantation and dispels the magic noose]

GHATOTKACHA Oh, the noose has fallen! What shall I do now? I see. Sir, remember your pledge.

BHIMA My pledge? I remember it. Go ahead.

[Both start going]

PRIEST My sons, what do we do? Bhima is going. Having defeated this fierce ogre, he is going like a bull sporting in the rain.

GHATOTKACHA Wait, I will inform my mother about your arrival.

BHIMA Very well. Go.

GHATOTKACHA (*Approaching*) Mother! I salute you. I have brought a man you were awaiting since long for your meal.

[Enter Hidimba]

HIDIMBA Live long, my son.

GHATOTKACHA I thank you.

HIDIMBA What kind of man have you brought, my son.

GHATOTKACHA Lady, he is a man only in appearance. In power he is more than a man.

HIDIMBA Is it a priest?

GHATOTKACHA Not a priest.

HIDIMBA Is it an old man?

GHATOTKACHA Not old.

HIDIMBA A child?

GHATOTKACHA Not a child.

HIDIMBA Let me see him.

[Both walk around]

HIDIMBA Is this the man you have brought?

GHATOTKACHA Who is he, mother?

HIDIMBA Idiot! He is our god.

GHATOTKACHA Whose god?

HIDIMBA Yours and mine!

GHATOTKACHA What is the proof?

HIDIMBA Here is the proof! Victory to you, noble one!

BHIMA (*Looking*) Who is that! The lady Hidimba? My lady you are a joy for this exile wandering in the forest. But who is this, Hidimba.

HIDIMBA (*In Bhima's ear*) It is thus, noble one.

BHIMA You are demon only by birth, not conduct.

HIDIMBA You crazy boy, salute your father.

GHATOTKACHA Father, I did not salute you earlier out of ignorance. Forgive your son's mistake. I, Ghatotkacha, doom of the sons of Dhritarashtra, salute you.

BHIMA Come, my son. You are forgiven indeed. (*Embracing*) He is the doom of the Kauravas. The hearts of fathers always long for their sons. May you be brave and strong, my son.

GHATOTKACHA I thank you.

PRIEST This is Ghatotkacha, the son of Bhimasena.

BHIMA Son, salute the reverend Keshava Dasa.

GHATOTKACHA I salute you, sir.

PRIEST May you be as virtuous and famous as your father.

GHATOTKACHA I thank you.

PRIEST O Bhima, you have protected my family and saved your own. Now we go.

BHIMA Our hermitage is not far from here, sir. Rest there and then go. All this has turned out well, thanks to your grace.

PRIEST You have already fulfilled the duties of a host by saving our lives. So, we will go.

BHIMA Go with your family, sir, till we meet again.

PRIEST That is a good thought. Very well.

[Exit Keshava Dasa with his wife and sons]

BHIMA This way, Hidimba. Ghatotkacha, my son, this way. Let us at least escort the reverend Keshava Dasa till the hermitage gate.

Epilogue

As the ocean is to the rivers, as fire is to flames,
as is the mind to the senses,
so to us all is Lord Hari, our Lord.

[Exit all]

Five Nights

Pancharātram

{2}

Five Nights

Pancharātram

This play is based on a well-known episode in the *Mahābhārata*, but makes significant departures from it to create its own dramatic story. The dramatist would have expected his audience to be familiar with the original episode in the epic, which is recounted here in brief.

The Pandava king Yudhishthira lost his kingdom in a game of dice with his cousins and enemies, the Kauravas, and was forced into exile along with his four brothers and their common queen Draupadi. A condition of the exile was that its thirteenth and final year should be spent in hiding: if the Pandavas were discovered before this year ended, they would be obliged to repeat another twelve years in exile.

In the thirteenth year the Pandavas disguised themselves as former retainers in the court of Yudhishthira, and entered the service of Virata, king of Matsya: Yudhishthira as the king's companion; Bhimasena as the royal cook; Arjuna as a eunuch instructor of dance to the king's daughter, and the twin sons of queen Madri, Nakula and Sahdeva, respectively as a groom and a cowherd. Draupadi was employed as an attendant to the queen of Matsya.

Kichaka, the brother of the Matsya queen, became infatuated with Draupadi. Eventually, to escape his unwelcome attention she accepted a rendezvous with him where he was killed by Bhima.

Thereafter his kinsmen wished to lynch Draupadi, but Bhima killed them also. The news of these killings reached the Kauravas who suspected that it may lead them to the discovery of the hidden Pandavas. They mounted a cattle raid on the Matsya kingdom expecting that this would lead the Pandavas to reveal themselves.

When the news of this raid reached King Virata's capital, he and his retainers were away on other business, and only his young son Uttara was at home. Urged by Draupadi, this prince went forth to stop the raiders, accompanied by Arjuna, disguised as the eunuch Brihannala, as his charioteer.

When Uttara saw the Kaurava hosts, he took fright and wanted to run away. But, the eunuch drove his chariot instead to a cremation ground where the Pandavas had hidden their weapons. There Arjuna revealed himself to the prince, took charge of the battle, and promptly routed the Kauravas.

On his return to the capital, Arjuna was still in disguise as Brihannala, and attempted to credit Prince Uttara with the victory. But the latter proclaimed his identity, and that of the other Pandavas also became known. Coincidentally, the period of exile had also ended. Virata offered the hand of his daughter Uttarā to Arjuna, but he declined it for the honourable reason that, as his pupil, she was like a daughter to him. Instead he accepted her for his son Abhimanyu. The marriage was celebrated with great fanfare. It was also a step in the creation of an alliance by the Pandavas for regaining their kingdom from the Kauravas, which would ultimately lead to war.

Bhasa has in his own way embroidered this story in the present play. In its first act, the Kaurava chief Duryodhana, in good spirits after a great sacrificial ceremony, promises his preceptor Drona that he will restore their kingdom to the Pandavas, provided they can be discovered within the next five nights. Drona is also the preceptor of the Pandavas, and an advocate of their cause. He accepts Duryodhana's condition on the advice of Bhishma, the grand-uncle of both the Kauravas and the Pandavas, who infers from the news of Kichaka's death in Matsya about the Pandavas' presence there, and further suggests a cattle raid to enable their discovery. The story told in this act does not exist in the original epic.

The second act features the cattle raid and its aftermath. Arjuna's son Abhimanyu, participates on the Kaurava side in the raid and is captured by his uncle Bhima and produced in the court of Virata in a dramatic scene. Abhimanyu could well have been with the Kauravas as he was not in exile, had attended the sacrificial ceremony of Duryodhana who was also his uncle twice removed, and may have been prepared to join his kinsmen in a raid on enemies. But this episode also does not exist in the *Mahābhārata*.

In the final act, the Kaurava side is depicted as expressing deep concern at the capture of Abhimanyu. Duryodhana himself plans to get him released, implying that his differences with the Pandavas are a family quarrel not brooking of outside interference. In a series of vivid descriptions it then becomes clear that the Pandavas have been discovered, and Drona holds Duryodhana to his promise of the five nights. Duryodhana agrees to return their kingdom to the Pandavas and the play ends on a happy note. This act, of course, is also Bhasa's invention: it makes unnecessary the war which is the central theme of the epic.

In accordance with convention, the combats in the play involving Arjuna and Abhimanyu do not take place on stage. They are instead described with great effect in dialogues between third parties. The sacrificial ceremony is also described in detail in a conversation between three priests in the conventional interlude at the beginning of the play. In view of its length and the somewhat repetitive nature of the description which is not relevant to the subsequent action, this interlude has bene abridged slightly in the present translation.

Bhasa depicts some of the characters in this play in a new

light as compared to their traditional presentation in the epic. Duryodhana is essentially noble, magnanimous, true to his word and with a strong sense of family loyalty. His friend Karna is a loyal adviser urging the path of virtue. His maternal uncle, Shakuni, is not as wicked as he appears in the *Mahābhārata*. The patriarch Bhishma is a somewhat wily old man.

A large number of characters are mentioned in the play in different contexts. There are references to the main figures of the *Rāmāyana*, to Rama and his ancestor Ikshvaku as examples of ideal kingship, and to the discovery of Rama's abducted wife Sita by the monkey-god Hanuman. Another reference is to Jarasandha, a mighty king and friend of the Kauravas, who was killed by Bhima in single combat. His son Sahadeva attended Duryodhan's sacrifice. Bhishmaka and Bhurishrava are other kings present there. Ashwatthama, Kripa and Jayadaratha were noted warriors on the Kaurava side. Vidura was the half-brother and close adviser of Duryodhan's father. Parashu Rama, a warrior-sage, and Balarama, the brother of Krishna, are mentioned as the equals of Bhima in physical prowess. Krishna himself is mentioned as the uncle of Abhimanyu: his sister was the wife of Arjuna, and Abhimanyu's mother. Duhshasana, the younger brother of Duryodhana had humiliated the queen Draupadi at the game of dice and was on this account a particular *bete noir* of her husbands, the Pandava princes.

The mention of the house of lac refers to the conspiracy in which Duryodhana attempted to incinerate the Pandavas. The reference to the Khandava forest concerns an episode in the *Mahābhārata* in which Arjuna displayed his skill as an archer by shooting a net of arrows over that forest to prevent rain from falling on it.

Eunuchs at the time of the play, as also in later days, wore women's clothes and were referred to in the feminine gender. Like most women they spoke in the vernacular Prakrit rather than in classical Sanskrit. But warfare was too important to be described in Prakrit, and hence the king's instruction to Brihannala to describe it in Sanskrit, the language of the court.

The benedictory verse at the beginning of this play is an example of paronomasia in the original text. Playing on other meanings of the relevant proper nouns, it both invokes divine blessings and also introduces the main characters of the play. Literally, it calls for protection from the one who is resplendent (*viraj*), the earth's cloud (*drona*) messenger, pure (*arjuna*) and formidable (*bhima*), the navigator (*karnadhara*), of the lord of birds (*shakuni*), the one hard to fight (*duryodhana*), the terrible (*bhishma*) and firm in combat (*yudhishthira*), the follower of the higher (*uttara*) path and intent on sacrifice (*abhimanyu*). The sense obviously is that the same divinity is immanent in all the dramatic characters so named, and this is what has been conveyed in the translation. That the deity addressed is Vishnu is clear from the expression 'lord of birds', an epithet for his divine eagle, Garuda.

Cast in order of appearance

The Producer	*in the Prologue*
Three Priests	*in the interlude*
Drona	*the royal preceptor*
Bhishma	*grandsire of the Kuru clan*
Duryodhana	*king of the Kurus*
Karna	*lord of Anga, friend of Duryodhana*
Shakuni	*lord of Gandhara, Duryodhana's uncle*
An old cowherd	*of Matsya*
Gomitraka	*another cowherd*
The King	*Virata of Matsya*
Bhagavan	*the Pandava king, Yudhishthira, disguised as a priest and companion of Virata*
Brihannala	*his brother Arjuna, disguised as a eunuch*
Bhimasena	*his brother, also in disguise*
Abhimanyu	*son of Arjuna, nephew of Duryodhana*
Uttara	*son of Virata*

Also soldiers, charioteers, envoys, cowherds and maids.

Prologue

[After the benediction, enter the Producer]

PRODUCER May he protect us all: he whose names are Bhishma and Drona, Karna and Arjuna, Duryodhana and Bhima, Yudhishthira and Shakuni, Uttara, Virata as well as Abhimanyu. (*Moves about*) And now, distinguished spectators, I have to announce that—but what is that? There seems to be a sound just as I was about to start. Well, let me see.

[Voices off stage]

VOICES How splendid is the Kuru king's sacrifice . . .

PRODUCER Ah, I see. Duryodhana, the king of the Kurus, is holding a ceremonial sacrifice. And all the other princes have assembled there with their families to honour him.

[Exit]

[END OF PROLOGUE]

Interlude

[Enter Three Priests]

ALL How splendid is the Kuru king's sacrifice.

FIRST The ritual grain scattered by the priests looks like flowers blooming everywhere. The scented smoke of sacrifice surpasses the fragrance of flowering trees. Tigers have become gentle like deer. Lions have ceased hunting in the hills. It seems that all the world has been initiated into the sacred ceremony with the king.

SECOND Well said, sir. All the world is happy at this moment. The sacred fire representing the gods is sated with oblations. The priests are sated with gifts. All men and beasts and birds are content. They all proclaim the merits of the king. The merits of such a king make this earth surpass heaven.

THIRD Look at these venerable priests. Staves in hand and supported by their disciples, they move slowly like aged elephants. Their austerities have increased with age. Their ears and mouths are accustomed to the chant of scriptures and their feet to the salute of royal turbans.

FIRST Oh! The king of the Kurus, Duryodhana, is coming this way. He is accompanied by all the illustrious princes led by Bhishma and Drona. With sweet words, they tell him, 'Conquer and nourish the earth with the power of sacrifice. Be kind to your kinsmen. Give up anger.' They support the Pandavas. Come, let us also greet the Kuru king.

OTHER TWO Very well.

ALL Victory! Victory to Your Majesty. (*Exit*)

[END OF INTERLUDE]

ACT I

[Enter Bhishma and Drona]

DRONA Duryodhana has gratified me with his piety. For the faults of a student are laid at the door of his teacher, not of his friends or relations. His parents are not held responsible for them either, as they entrust the students to the preceptor from childhood.

BHISHMA Acquisition made Duryodhana prosperous. Belligerence made him notorious. But piety and good deeds have given him glory.

[Enter Duryodhana, with Karna and Shakuni]

DURYODHANA My heart is full of faith. My elders are pleased. The world acknowledges my virtues. My reputation is untarnished. It is not true that people go to heaven only after death. For me heaven is here itself.

KARNA Son of Gandhari, you earned your wealth lawfully, and you have spent it according to the law. The warrior's wealth depends upon his arms. To hoard it for his children is not the warrior's way. A king should donate all his wealth for sacred tasks, and leave only his sword for his son.

SHAKUNI Well said, prince of Anga.

KARNA Ikshvaku and Rama, and all the other kings of old have passed away. So have their treasures and their kingdoms. They live on only through the fame of their sacrifices.

ALL Son of Gandhari, congratulations on the sacrifice and your success.

DURYODHANA I thank you. Preceptor, my salutations.

DRONA Come, my child. But that is not in order.

DURYODHANA Why, what is the order?

DRONA Don't you see, sir? You should first salute the blessed Bhishma. I don't consider it in order to be saluted before him.

BHISHMA No, no, sir. You have precedence over me for many reasons. I am born of a mother, your birth was immaculate; my profession is arms, yours is compassion; I am a warrior, you a priest; and you are the preceptor, I am only the first among the disciples.

DRONA The truly great are always averse to self-praise. Come then, child, salute me.

DURYODHANA Preceptor, I salute you.

DRONA My child, may you always enjoy the fatigue of a sacrifice well performed.

DURYODHANA I thank you. Grandfather, I salute you.

BHISHMA Grandson, may your mind always be tranquil like this.

DURYODHANA I thank you. Uncle, I salute you.

SHAKUNI Child, may you perform all the sacrifices thus, giving away great gifts. And, like Jarasandha, may you vanquish all the kings and bring them to the royal sacrifice in chains.

DRONA Oh! Shakuni incites even in his benedictions. This warrior prince has no time for peace.

DURYODHANA Karna, my friend. After saluting the elders, the time has come to embrace friends.

KARNA Son of Gandhari, your body is worn out with sacrificial fasting. I wonder if it can bear the strength of my embrace. So I will only speak of my affection. Besides, I am afraid of you, now that you have become a royal sage!

DURYODHANA May you always be like this.

DRONA Duryodhana, my son, here is Bhishmaka the friend of Indra, who congratulates you.

DURYODHANA Welcome sir. My greetings.

BHISHMA Grandson Duryodhana, here is Bhurishrava, the guardian of the southern lands, who congratulates you.

DURYODHANA Welcome, sir.

DRONA Son, here is Abhimanyu, who has been sent by Krishna to congratulate you.

SHAKUNI Duryodhana, here is Sahadeva, the son of Jarasandha, who greets you.

DURYODHANA Welcome my lad, may you be glorious like your father.

ALL Here are all the kings to congratulate you.

DURYODHANA I thank you all. But how is it that while all the kings have come here, Virata has not come?

SHAKUNI I had sent an emissary to him. Perhaps he is on his way.

DURYODHANA Preceptor, you have taught me both my duties and the art of war. Please accept the fee due to the preceptor.

DRONA The due fee? Let it be. I will ask for it another time.

DURYODHANA The preceptor does not need to ask.

BHISHMA What is the need for it. He has received the libations of sacrifice since childhood. He has enjoyed your hospitality. He has earned fame. There is nothing special which this preceptor of princes lacks.

DURYODHANA Command me, sir. What do you wish for? What should I do?

DRONA Duryodhana! My son! I will tell you.

DURYODHANA Now what are you thinking of, sir? I know I am dearer to you than life. You have made me. I am counted among the true warriors. I can dare. Tell me freely what you wish and what I should give. Let the mace alone remain in my hands, everything else is at your disposal.

DRONA I would tell you son, only tears prevent me.

ALL What is it? The preceptor is weeping!

BHISHMA Grandson Duryodhana, your efforts are in vain.

DURYODHANA Ho, there!

[Enter a Soldier]

SOLDIER Victory to the king.

DURYODHANA Some water.

SOLDIER As the king commands. (*Exits and re-enters*) Victory to the king. Here is the water.

DURYODHANA Give it to me. (*Taking the jar*) Preceptor, please wash the tears from your face.

DRONA Let it be. Doing my duty will be enough.

DURYODHANA Alas if you are thinking of my past wickedness, if you are thinking that I will not give what you ask for. Give me your hand, hard as an arrowhead. Let this water be the guarantee of my gift.

DRONA O my heart believes you. Listen, my son. Divide the kingdom with the homeless Pandavas who have been in exile for twelve years. This is my request. This will be my due fee.

SHAKUNI (*Excitedly*) Wait a minute, sir! Your disciple pledged himself, trusting in your status as his preceptor. Is it proper to make such a proposal at his sacrifice? Is it not trickery in the name of duty?

DRONA How is it trickery in the name of duty? You are too proud of Gandhara, Shakuni. You think everyone is as ignoble as you are. Is it trickery to ask that brothers be given back their ancestral kingdom? Is it not better to give it back on their request, than that they should seize it by force?

ALL How by force?

BHISHMA Grandson Duryodhana! You have just completed a ritual sacrifice. Shakuni speaks like your friend, but actually he is your enemy. Do not listen to him. Look, grandson, the

Pandavas and Draupadi wander through forests covered with grime. If you have turned against them, and they against you, it is all because of Shakuni's harsh pride.

DURYODHANA It may be, but I ask you, preceptor . . .

DRONA Speak, son.

DURYODHANA If they are capable of force, why didn't they do anything at the time when they were deprived of their honour and their kingdom in front of everyone?

DRONA This should be asked of Yudhishthira who likes to gamble and was tricked by duty. It was he who prevented Bhima from pulling down the pillars of the assembly hall. Had he done so, perhaps Shakuni would not be here to revile us.

BHISHMA What were we seeking, and what have we got? Preceptor, our work is more important than this quarrel.

DRONA This is not the time for grovelling. Better quarrel if we must.

BHISHMA Your pardon, preceptor. Look, grandson, they are weak, homeless and downtrodden. They humbly seek friendship. They love you. You are the elder. Will you have them in your family, or should they wander with the beasts?

SHAKUNI Let them wander. Let them wander.

KARNA Do not be angry, preceptor. You know that Duryodhana cannot bear harsh words even if they are meant for his good. He does not like others praised before him. Help him do the disciple's duty at the end of the sacrifice. A wayward elephant must be ridden gently.

DRONA Dear Karna! Priests can sometimes be overpowering. You have reminded me in time. I take your point. Duryodhana, my child, do I have any claim on you?

BHISHMA Now he is on the right path. The wilful need gentle treatment.

DURYODHANA Not only on me, sir, on my entire family.

DRONA That is well said, son. If I deceive you, the fault will not be yours. If I press you, you will be the gainer. Differences within great families can be resolved with the advice of preceptors.

DURYODHANA I would like some more advice on this.

DRONA Whose advice do you want, son? Bhishma, Karna, Kripa, Vidura, Ashwatthama, Jayadratha the king of Sindhu, your father, your mother? Tell me, son, whose advice?

DURYODHANA No, I want it from uncle.

DRONA From uncle! (*Aside*) O this will spoil everything.

DURYODHANA Uncle, please come here. Friend Karna, come here please.

DRONA (*Aside*) Well, I must do this. (*To Shakuni*) Lord of Gandhara, my child, come here please.

SHAKUNI Here I am.

DRONA My child, old men are prone to anger. They are impulsive like children. They should be forgiven. To make up for my harsh words, here is my embrace.

BHISHMA (*Aside*) Out of love for his disciple, the preceptor is trying to placate Shakuni. But Shakuni is too wicked for that.

SHAKUNI (*Aside*) The preceptor is a rogue. He is trying to placate me for his own purposes.

[All walk around, and sit]

DURYODHANA Uncle, what is your decision about giving half the kingdom to the Pandavas.

SHAKUNI My decided view is that it should not be given.

DURYODHANA It would be more worthy to say that it should be given, uncle.

SHAKUNI If it is to be given, then why consult us. Give away the whole kingdom.

DURYODHANA Friend Karna, you have not said anything?

KARNA What shall I say? I cannot oppose good brotherhood which Rama himself observed and promoted in the past. To give or not to give is your decision. We stand by you, even if there is war.

DURYODHANA Uncle, think of some inhospitable land, infertile and full of powerful and unfriendly people, which may be given to the Pandavas to live in.

SHAKUNI There is no such land. Who is more powerful than Arjuna? And even barren land will yield harvests if Yudhishthira rules over it.

DURYODHANA Well, lord of Gandhara, now I have poured water in the preceptor's palm. It is the proof of a pledge, as the elders know. I may have been tricked, I may have been impolitic, or it may be anything else. But I wish to honour that pledge. That water must be true.

SHAKUNI You have to be saved from perjury. Isn't it that, sir?

DURYODHANA What else?

SHAKUNI Then come here. (*Approaching Drona*) O preceptor, His Majesty the king of the Kurus wishes to inform you.

DRONA My child! Lord of Gandhara! Please speak on.

SHAKUNI If the whereabouts of the Pandavas can be discovered within five nights, he will give them half the kingdom. Now you must find them, sir.

DRONA Not like that, sir. You all have not been able to find them for twelve years despite all your efforts and tricks. How will I find them within five nights? It is better to say clearly that my fee will not be given.

BHISHMA Duryodhana! In duty there is no place for deception, grandson! We are all pleased with your intention. Whether it is now or later, give the Pandavas their share and fulfil your pledge. The Kurus always keep their word.

DURYODHANA That indeed is my intention.

DRONA (*To himself*) To serve my purpose, I wish today I was Hanuman who crossed the ocean and discovered the lost Sita in a moment. Now from where can one get news of the Pandavas.

[Enter a Soldier]

SOLDIER Victory to the king. An envoy has arrived from the city of Matsya.

ALL Bring him in quickly.

SOLDIER As you command. (*Exit*)

[Enter the Envoy]

ENVOY Victory to the king.

ALL Is King Virata coming?

ENVOY He is bereaved and cannot come.

ALL What has happened?

ENVOY May it please Your Majesty. His close relatives, the hundred Kichaka brothers, were secretly killed by someone last night. With bare hands it seems, for there was no sign on their bodies that the murder had been committed with any weapon.

ALL How could they be killed without a weapon?

BHISHMA Without a weapon? (*Aside*) Preceptor, accept the condition of the five nights.

DRONA (*Aside*) What do you mean?

BHISHMA This is obviously the work of Bhimasena's mighty arms. His anger with these hundred brothers has descended upon those hundred.

DRONA How do you know, sir?

BHISHMA Come, priest, how can old bulls not know the horn marks of their frisky calves as they gambol on the river bank?

DRONA Old bulls? Ah, I see. My work is done. (*To Duryodhana*) Duryodhana, my son, I accept the five nights.

DURYODHANA What? You accept the five nights?

DRONA O you kings who have come to witness this sacrifice! Listen to me! His Majesty Duryodhana, the king of the Kurus—no, no, the king together with his uncle—accepts that he will give half the kingdom to the Pandavas if they are discovered. Isn't that so, my son?

DURYODHANA That is so.

DRONA Please consider this once or twice again.

SHAKUNI I will consider it at the appropriate time.

DRONA Bhishma?

BHISHMA (*Aside*) The preceptor cannot contain his joy. I fear that he may have been tricked rather than Duryodhana. (*To Duryodhana*) Grandson, Virata has a hidden enmity with me. He has not come to witness this sacrifice. Therefore, we should seize his cattle.

DRONA (*Aside*) O Bhishma! King Virata is a dear disciple of mine. How can we seize his cattle.

BHISHMA (*Aside*) You simple priest! The rumble of war chariots will certainly provoke the Pandavas' wrath. They are grateful people. Seizing the cattle will serve our purpose.

SOLDIER Victory to the king. The chariots are ready for going back to the city.

DURYODHANA Let us go in these very chariots to seize his cattle. Let my hands once more wield the mace which lay passive during the sacrifice.

DRONA Let my chariot be called.

SHAKUNI Bring my elephant.

KARNA Bring the chariot yoked with strong horses.

BHISHMA Bring my bow quickly. I cannot wait to reach the city of King Virata.

ALL Leave your bow and stay here, sir. We will carry out your commands.

DRONA Duryodhana, my son, both of us wish to see your prowess in battle.

DURYODHANA As you wish, sir.

DRONA Lord of Gandhara, my child, your chariot will be at the head of this expedition.

SHAKUNI Very well. This is a good idea.

[Exit all]

ACT II

[Enter an old cowherd]

OLD COWHERD May my cows have many calves. May the cowherdesses never be widowed. May our king Virata have sovereign dominion. We are here in this orchard near the city for the celebration of King Virata's birthday. The cowherds and maids and all the cattle are enjoying themselves. And I will receive the honours due to the elders. (*Looking*) But why is that crow, perched on a leafless tree, and sharpening its beak against a dry branch, screaming towards the sun? God protect us and our cattle. Now, as the eldest, I must call the boys and girls. (*Moves around*) Gomitraka! O Gomitraka!

GOMITRAKA Uncle! Salutations.

OLD COWHERD May god protect us and our cattle. The cowherds and maids and all the cattle who have come to this orchard for the celebration of King Virata's birthday are enjoying themselves. O Gomitraka, call the boys and girls.

GOMITRAK As you say, uncle. Ho! Gorakshinika! Ghritapinda! Swamini! Vrishabha Dutta! Kumbha Dutta! Mahisha Dutta! Come! Come quickly!

[Enter all]

ALL Uncle, we salute you.

OLD COWHERD May God protect our cattle and all you boys and girls. The cattle have come to this orchard for the celebration of King Virata's birthday. Let us sing and dance till then.

ALL As you say, uncle.

[All dance]

OLD COWHERD Haha! Well danced! Well sung! I will also dance. (*Dances*).

ALL Oh! Oh! Uncle! What a lot of dust has been raised.

OLD COWHERD It is not only dust! There is the sound of bugles and conch-shells.

ALL Oh uncle! The dust has covered the sun. It looks pale like the moon in daylight.

GOMITRAKA O uncle! Some people riding in horse carts with white sunshades are rounding up our herd, the thieves.

OLD COWHERD O there is a shower of arrows. Boys! Girls! Get into the huts quickly.

ALL As you say, uncle.

[Exit]

OLD COWHERD O wait, wait! Strike, strike! Catch them! I will report this to King Virata! (*Exit*)

[Enter a Soldier]

SOLDIER Let it be known! Let it be known to the king that the sons of Dhritarashtra, their valour changed into banditry, are stealing our cows. The calves have stampeded. The cows are berserk. The bulls are frightened. There is commotion everywhere. The herd is in a desperate condition.

[Voice backstage]

VOICE Is it the sons of Dhritarashtra?

SOLDIER What else, sir.

[Enter a Chamberlain]

CHAMBERLAIN It is to be expected from those who oppress even their own kinsmen. Mounted on chariots, clad in armour and archer's habit, their bows drawn ready for battle, they are taking out their enmity with our king on these poor cows.

Jayasena, the king is busy with the ceremonies of his birth

anniversary. This is not the time to inform him, for he may get angry. So I will inform him when the benedictions are over.

SOLDIER Sir, this matter brooks no delay. Inform him quickly.

CHAMBERLAIN He will be informed just now.

[Enter the King]

KING Shame on this hand of mine. Perfumed and bejewelled, it enjoys delicacies while my cows are stolen and their calves scared and scattered by the roar of chariots. Jayasena! Jayasena!

SOLDIER Victory, victory to the king.

KING Enough of that. My kingship has been insulted. Tell me the details of the battle.

SOLDIER Your Majesty, unpleasant things do not deserve to be recounted in detail. In brief, the dust of the chariots covered all the cattle. The whip alone distinguished them, one from the other.

KING Then quickly bring my bow and ready my chariot. Let whoever loves me, follow me freely. To defend the cows in battle is never fruitless. Death will bring fame. And to secure their release will give merit.

SOLDIER As the king commands. (*Exit*)

KING What indeed could be the cause of Duryodhana's enmity with me? That I did not go to attend his sacrifice? But how could I attend? We were in mourning at the death of the Kichakas. Or, he may think that we support the Pandavas secretly. In any case, we must fight. Bhagavan knows the ways of Duryodhana from his time at Hastinapura. He will certainly not reveal Duryodhana's weaknesses. But those in need must nevertheless ask. Who's there?

[Enter a Soldier]

SOLDIER Victory to the king.

KING Please call Bhagavan.

SOLDIER As the king commands. (*Exit*)

[Enter Bhagavan]

BHAGAVAN (*Looking around*) O what is this? War-elephants are being readied and war-horses dressed in armour; chariots are being yoked and warriors girding for battle. Seeing these preparations, I am touched by an unknown fear. I am sure of myself but the others are impulsive. (*Approaching*) Sir, may you be victorious.

KING Sir, Virata greets you.

BHAGAVAN May you be fortunate.

KING Thank you. Here is a chair. Please take a seat.

BHAGAVAN Very well. (*Sits down*) O king, why these preparations? Are you not content with your present frontiers? Or do you intend to put down the insolent or liberate the oppressed?

KING Bhagavan, my cattle has been seized and I have been insulted.

BHAGAVAN By whom?

KING By the sons of Dhritarashtra.

BHAGAVAN By the sons of Dhritarashtra? (*Aside*) Alas! Ties of kinship colour the minds even of thinking people. They commit a crime, and we feel guilty.

KING What are you thinking, Bhagavan?

BHAGAVAN Nothing. I am worried for them.

KING They will be put in their place today. Yudhishthira may have forgiven them, despite his power. I cannot.

BHAGAVAN Even so. (*Aside*) Now it is all admirable: the loss of kingdom, the humiliation of Draupadi, the living in disguise as dependants, the bed of leaves on the floor. For he considers it my forgiveness.

[Enter a Soldier]

SOLDIER Victory to the king.

KING Now what is Duryodhana up to?

SOLDIER It is not only Duryodhana. All the mighty warriors are there. Bhishma and Drona, Jayadratha and Shalya, Karna and

Shakuni and Kripa. Leave aside their arrows. The standards and banners waving on their chariots have alone repulsed us.

KING (*Rising up with hands joined in salutation*) What? Even the lord Bhishma is there?

BHAGAVAN (*Aside*) It is admirable that even though wronged, the king does not fail in courtesy. But why has the grandsire of the Kurus come at this time? I suspect it is to remind me that our period of exile is over.

KING Who is there?

[Enter a Soldier]

SOLDIER Victory to the king.

KING Call my charioteer.

SOLDIER As the king commands. (*Exit*)

[Enter the Charioteer]

CHARIOTEER Victory and long life, master.

KING Bring my chariot quickly. We have a respected guest for battle. I will welcome Bhishma with arrows though it may be too much to hope that I will win.

CHARIOTEER As the master commands. But master, the chariot which you use for subduing enemies has been taken away by Prince Uttara to display his own prowess in battle.

KING The prince has gone? How?

BHAGAVAN Stop the prince, O king! Stop him. I do not mean him any disrespect in telling you of the dangers of battle. The fire of battle is fierce and uncertain. It is no respecter of persons. Neither are the sons of Dhritarashtra.

KING Then prepare another chariot quickly.

CHARIOTEER As you command, master.

KING But . . . just come here.

CHARIOTEER Here I am, master.

KING Why did you not drive the prince's chariot? You are the royal charioteer, sir. Did he not permit you?

CHARIOTEER I beg your pardon, master. Indeed I prepared the

chariot and presented myself. But the prince ignored me and appointed Brihannala as the charioteer. Whether to mock her or whether because of her competence, I do not know.

KING Brihannala? How . . .

BHAGAVAN O king, there is no need to worry. If Brihannala has gone with your chariot, then the thunder of its wheels alone will be enough to disperse the enemy. It will return victorious in no time.

KING Then prepare another chariot quickly.

CHARIOTEER As the master commands. (*Exit*)

[Enter a Soldier]

SOLDIER The prince's chariot has been repulsed.

KING Repulsed? How?

BHAGAVAN Repulsed? At this time?

SOLDIER May it please Your Majesty. Many enemy warriors confronted the horses. So the chariot was repulsed. It turned towards the cremation ground to seek refuge in the forest.

BHAGAVAN (*Aside*) Ah that is where the Gandiva bow is hidden. (*To the king*) Your Majesty, that the chariot turned towards the cremation ground is an omen. It means that the place where the sons of Dhritarashtra stand will become their own cremation ground.

KING Bhagavan! This is no time for soothsaying. It only irritates.

BHAGAVAN There is no need for irritation. I have never made a false prediction.

KING That is so. Well, go once more and find out what is happening.

SOLDIER As the king commands. (*Exit*)

KING From where comes that sudden sound, making the earth tremble, like a river bursting its banks. Find out what it is.

[Enter a Soldier]

SOLDIER Victory to the king. The prince rested his horses for some moments at the cremation ground. And then . . . .

BHAGAVAN I hope this will not make me a false prophet.

KING What did the prince do?

SOLDIER He made the dark elephants red with showers of arrows. There was not a horse or a warrior which escaped his arrows. The chariots too were silenced with arrows. A river of arrows flowed from his terrible bow.

BHAGAVAN (*Aside*) That can only be the bow whose arrows matched the rain that Indra poured on the Khandava forest.

KING And what news of the enemy?

SOLDIER I did not see it with my own eyes. But those who did say that when Drona heard the sound of that bow, he realized whose it was and simply turned back. When Bhishma saw the arrow hit his standard, he just put down his weapons. Karna was repulsed by the arrows, and the other princes were as if spellbound at what had happened. Only the boy Abhimanyu did not succumb to fear but fought on.

BHAGAVAN How is Abhimanyu here? Your Majesty, if he is in the battle, please send another charioteer, for Brihannala will not be able to cope with the fiery power of Abhimanyu.

KING No, sir, not so. Even Parashu Rama was no match for Bhishma. And Drona has divine weapons. Having repulsed them both, and also Karna and Jayadratha and the others, will the prince not be able to deal with Abhimanyu? Or, out of consideration for Abhimanyu's father they may become friends. They are of the same age. (*To the soldier*) Go, get the news again.

SOLDIER As the king commands. (*Exit and re-enters*) Victory to the king. Victory to the lord Virata. I have good news. The cattle raid has been repulsed. The sons of Dhritarashtra have fled.

BHAGAVAN Congratulations, Your Majesty.

KING Congratulations to you. And where is the prince now?

SOLDIER The prince is reviewing the soldiers who displayed bravery in battle.

KING That is admirable. The agony of wounded soldiers is relieved if their bravery in battle is immediately recognized. And where is Brihannala?

SOLDIER She has gone inside to give the good news.

KING Well, send for Brihannala.

SOLDIER As the king commands. (*Exit*)

[Enter Brihannala]

BRIHANNALA (*Looking around, aside*) Living as a woman had put me out of practice. I had to struggle a bit to string the bow, Gandiv. My grip on the arrows was not firm. The arm guard kept slipping. But the old skills returned quickly. It was embarrassing to draw the bow before all those princes in this dress. But they were soon covered with a hail of arrows and bit the dust. Well, I have rescued the cattle and won a victory for the king. But I feel no joy in this victory, as I did not seize Duhshasana in the battle today and lead him captive to the city of King Virata. I feel embarrassed to go before the king wearing these jewels presented so lovingly by Uttarā. But I must see the lord Virata. (*Walks around and looks*) Oh, here is the noble Yudhishthira. A king, he is disguised here as a priest. Instead of a sceptre he carries a staff. But he is glorious even without his kingdom. (*Approaching*) Bhagavan, I salute you.

BHAGAVAN Bless you.

BRIHANNALA Victory to the master.

KING Brihannala has earned great respect. For high or low, it is deeds which matter, not appearance or family. Brihannala, you must be tired, but still I will trouble you. Tell us about the battle in detail.

BRHIHANNALA Listen, master.

KING These were brave deeds. Recount them in the language of the court.

BRIHANNALA May it please Your Majesty . . .

[Enter a Soldier]

SOLDIER Victory to the king.

KING Your joy seems exceptional. Why are you so excited?

SOLDIER There is unbelievable good news. Abhimanyu has been taken prisoner.

BRIHANNALA Taken prisoner? How? (*Aside*) I reviewed our warriors today. I also saw him in battle. There is none to compare with him from this side, now that the Kichakas are dead.

BHAGAVAN Brihannala, what are you thinking?

BRIHANNALA Bhagavan, I do not know who captured him. He is strong and well-trained. Perhaps the ill luck of his father led to his capture.

KING Well, how was he captured?

SOLDIER By one who fearlessly climbed on to the chariot, gathered him in his arms, and brought him down.

KING Who?

SOLDIER He whom the king has appointed in the kitchen.

BRIHANNALA (*Aside*) So, he was not captured. He was embraced by the noble Bhima. The rest of us were content to get a glimpse of him from afar. But Bhima gave vent to his affection in front of everyone.

KING Accord all honour to Abhimanyu, and bring him here.

BHAGAVAN Your Majesty, people will think that you are giving honours to Abhimanyu because you are afraid that he is protected by the Yadavas and the Pandavas. It will be better not to accord him any honour.

KING Abhimanyu cannot be treated without honours. He is the heir of Yudhishthira. Because of my family connections with Drupada he is like a grandson to me. Besides, he is of the same age as my own son, and could be a son-in-law as I have a daughter. Guests deserve to be honoured in any case. And the Pandavas are dear to me.

BHAGAVAN Well said. My words are taken back.

KING Well, who will bring Abhimanyu?

BHAGAVAN He can be brought by Brihannala.

KING Brihannala, please bring Abhimanyu here.

BRIHANNALA As the king commands. (*Aside*) This is one order I long for. (*Exit*)

BHAGAVAN Now he can see his son. In private he can embrace him and shed tears of joy. He would have been ashamed to do so in front of me.

KING Look at what the prince has accomplished. Bhishma and the others were defeated. Abhimanyu was captured. Uttara has had a truly great victory.

[Enter Bhimasena]

BHEEMASENA I had carried my mother and all my brothers in my arms out of the burning house of lac. When I brought Abhimanyu alone out of the chariot today, the effort was no less. This way, prince, this way.

[Enter Abhimanyu and Brihannala]

ABHIMANYU O who is that, broad of chest and slight of waist, with mighty shoulders and thighs? He lifted me up with one arm alone, powerfully and yet so gently.

BRIHANNALA This way, prince, this way.

ABHIMANYU And who is this other? His attire is common but he exudes power. Women's ornaments look out of place on him. He seems like a god in the garb of a goddess.

BRIHANNALA (*Aside*) What have you done, sir? He will bear the stigma of capture in his first battle. His defeat will anger his uncle, Krishna. His mother Subhadra, already separated from her husband, will suffer even more. What can I say? You have sullied your own valour.

BHIMASENA Arjuna?

BRIHANNALA What else, he is Arjuna's son.

BHIMASENA (*Aside*) I understand all these consequences of his capture. Who can bear to see his son in the hands of the enemy? Even so, I brought him so that Draupadi may see him in her sorrow.

BRIHANNALA (*Aside*) I am eager to hear him speak. Please make him say something, sir.

BHIMASENA (*Aside*) Very well. Abhimanyu!

ABHIMANYU What do you mean, Abhimanyu!

BHIMASENA I seem to have annoyed him. You make him speak.

BRIHANNALA Abhimanyu!

ABHIMANYU What is this? My name is Abhimanyu. But do low people call princes by name? Are these the manners here, or is this being done to insult a prisoner?

BRIHANNALA Abhimanyu, is your mother well?

ABHIMANYU You ask about my mother? Are you King Yudhishthira or Bheemasena or Arjuna that you address me with such familiarity, asking about our ladies?

BRIHANNALA And Krishna, Abhimanyu. Is he well, too?

ABHIMANYU What? You also speak of that lord by name? What is this? Your relatives are all well.

[Both stare at each other]

ABHIMANYU Now why does he laugh as if to ridicule me?

BRIHANNALA Not at all. Arjuna is your father and Krishna is your uncle. You are young and well-trained in weapons. With all this, how proper was it for you to be taken prisoner in combat.

ABHIMANYU Enough of this nonsense! We are not given to self-praise in our family. Go and look at the arrows which struck your soldiers. They are all mine.

BRIHANNALA (*Aside*) He is right. There was not a warrior who escaped his arrows. Even I would have been wounded if I had not turned my chariot away. (*To Abhimanyu*) You speak big words. How did that mere foot-soldier capture you?

ABHIMANYU He captured me because he approached me unarmed. How could the son of Arjuna strike someone who had no weapon?

BHIMASENA (*Aside*) Arjuna is fortunate indeed to hear both father and son extolled in the same breath.

KING Hurry up! Hurry up with Abhimanyu.

BRIHANNALA This way, prince, this way. Here is the king. You may approach him.

ABHIMANYU Oh, whose king?

BRIHANNALA No, no, he is with the priest.

ABHIMANYU With the priest? (*Approaching*) Sir, I salute you.

BHAGAVAN Come, my child. May you be endowed with all the virtues of your father: with valour, steadfastness, decorum, mercy, friendliness to kinsfolk and prowess with the bow. And, if you wish, may you also have the virtues of your four uncles.

ABHIMANYU I thank you.

KING Come here, son. But you do not greet me. O he is a proud one, this warrior prince. I will cure his pride. Well, by whom was he captured?

BHIMASENA By me, Your Majesty.

ABHIMANYU Say also that you were unarmed.

BHIMASENA Peace. These arms and shoulders are my natural weapons. I rely on them in battle. It is the weak who use the bow.

ABHIMANYU No, sir. You are not my middle uncle to use such words. You are not that stainless warrior whose arms alone are an army.

BHAGAVAN Who is this middle uncle, my son?

ABHIMANYU Listen. But we do not argue with priests. It would be better if someone else were to speak.

KING Very well, son. You can respond to me. Who is this middle uncle?

ABHIMANYU Listen. It is he who put the noose of his arms around King Jarasandha's neck and did the deed which even Krishna could not accomplish.

[Enter Uttara]

UTTARA False praise is very painful. They praise me for this battle, and I praise them back. But at heart I am ashamed. (*Approaching*) Greetings, Bhagavan.

BHAGAVAN May you be fortunate.

UTTARA Father, I salute you.

KING Come, my son. May you live long. Have you honoured the warriors who fought well?

UTTARA They have been honoured. But you must honour the one who deserves it the most.

KING Who is that, son?

UTTARA Here. The noble Arjuna.

KING Arjuna? How?

UTTARA How? This noble one took his bow and quivers full of arrows from the cremation ground and defeated Bhishma and the other princes. He protected us.

KING Is that so?

BRIHANNALA Have mercy, Your Majesty. He is confused because of youth. He fought the battle but does not realize it. He did it all, but attributes it to another.

UTTARA There is no room for doubt. Look at the bow-string scars on his wrist. They have not disappeared even in twelve years.

KING Let us see.

BRIHANNALA If I am Arjuna, the Pandava who battled with the great god, then obviously this must be Bhimasena, and that King Yudhishthira.

KING O King Yudhishthira, Bhimasena, Arjuna, why don't you trust me! Very well. The time is up. Brihannala, please go inside.

BRIHANNALA As the king commands.

BHAGAVAN Arjuna, you must not go in. Our pledge of incognito exile has been fulfilled.

ARJUNA As you command, noble one.

KING My house has been honoured by the stay of the brave and true Pandavas, fulfilling their pledge.

ABHIMANYU These are my fathers. They did not get angry at my harsh words, but instead laughed and teased me. The cattle raid was lucky for me. It has brought me to them. (*To Bhimasena*) O father, out of ignorance I did not salute you earlier. Please forgive a son's mistake. (*Salutes him*)

BHIMASENA Come, my son. May you be valiant like your father.

ABHIMANYU I salute you, father.

ARJUNA My child! (*Embraces him*) This touch of my son's body, denied for thirteen years, fills my heart with joy. Son, salute the lord Virata.

ABHIMANYU I salute you.

KING My child, may you have the steadfastness of Yudhishthira, the strength of Bhima, the dexterity of Arjuna and the beauty and intellect of the sons of Madri. And may you obtain the fame of Krishna, the beloved of the world. (*Aside*) The relationship with Uttarā troubles me What should I do now? Well, I see. Who's there?

[Enter a Soldier]

SOLDIER Victory to the king.

KING Bring the water.

SOLDIER As Your Majesty commands. (*Exit and re-enters*) Here is the water.

KING (*Takes water in hand*) Arjuna! Accept Uttarā in return for your victory against the cattle raiders.

YUDHISHTHIRA Now the head must hang down.

ARJUNA (*Aside*) Why, he is testing my character. (*To king*) O king, I respected the ladies of your household like mothers. So I accept Uttarā for my son.

YUDHISHTHIRA Now the head can be held high.

KING Arjuna's chivalry is famous among warriors. He has observed it equally during his stay in my household. The stars are favourable today. Let the wedding be arranged today itself.

YUDHISHTHIRA Very well. Let us send Prince Uttara to grandsire Bhishma.

KING As you wish. Come this way, King Yudhishthira, the noble Bhima and Arjuna. Let us go inside, joyfully.

ALL Very well.

[Exit all]

ACT III

[Enter a Charioteer]

CHARIOTEER Ho there! Ho there! Inform all the warriors and their preceptor that Abhimanyu has been abducted. The fear of Krishna's discus was disregarded. The long-exiled Pandavas were ignored. The Kuru archers could not protect him. It is a matter of shame.

[Enter Bhishma and Drona]

DRONA Tell me, tell me, charioteer. Who has taken the warrior-son of my pupil? Who wants to face my missiles? Tell me of his valour, his weapons, his strength, so that I may direct my powerful arrows as messengers towards him?

BHISHMA Say, charioteer, say who captured the young elephant when the herd had fled? His only fault was that he did not know how to run away from battle. He tarried because of his youth.

[Enter Duryodhana, Karna and Shakuni]

DURYODHANA Speak, charioteer. Who has taken Abhimanyu? I myself will get him released. It is well known that there is a family quarrel between me and his fathers. Because of that people will blame me for his abduction. But the family quarrel is not the fault of the children. And he is my child first, and only then of the Pandavas.

KARNA Your words are full of affection, and most appropriate, son of Gandhari. But it is not out of fear of what people will say, that we must liberate him. It is because that child was taken prisoner in battle fighting for you, and we did not protect him. Otherwise, we should give up our weapons and retire to the forest.

SHAKUNI There are many to protect Abhimanyu. His liberation is certain. King Virata will himself release him, recalling that he is the son of Arjuna. Or he will release him because of Krishna, or out of fear of Balarama's anger. Or the mighty Bhima will destroy the enemies and bring him out.

DRONA Charioteer, tell us how he was captured. Did the chariot over-turn or the horses go out of control? Was the ground unsuitable for the chariot or did you make some mistake? Or were his arrows used up, or bow-string broken? These are the usual hazards of chariot-warriors. Of course he may have been overpowered by enemy arrows, but he is too well-trained for that.

CHARIOTEER Sir, he is the science of archery personified. What does he not know? He was raining arrows. Besides we had none of the troubles you have mentioned. My chariot was moving like a wheel of fire. But a single foot-soldier came upon it and held it.

ALL A foot-soldier?

DRONA And what was this foot-soldier like?

CHARIOTEER What shall I describe? His looks or his deeds?

BHISHMA Women are described by looks; men by prowess. So tell us about his prowess.

CHARIOTEER Sir!

DURYODHANA You do not have to praise anyone with big words. Speak plainly. I am not worried even if he was like the wind.

CHARIOTEER May it please the king. He crossed the horses with great speed and caught hold of the chariot. The horses strained with their necks extended. But the chariot could not move.

BHISHMA Then put down the weapons.

ALL Why?

BHISHMA Because if a speeding chariot was stopped with bare hands, be sure they are those of Bhima. In the past also he was on foot when he similarly defeated Jayadratha who was trying to abduct Draupadi.

DRONA Bhishma is right. I know his swiftness from the time he was my pupil. Once, on the archery field, at the very moment when he drew the bow-string to his ear and released a shaft, I told him that his head had shaken. At once he sped like an arrow himself and caught the shaft before it could reach the target.

SHAKUNI This is laughable! I ask you gentlemen, aren't there other heroes in the world, that you see the Pandavas everywhere? Or is it because they are so dear to you?

BHISHMA Lord of Gandhara, all this is based on inference. All of us go to battle mounted on chariots, with bows and other weapons. There are only two, Balarama and Bhima, who fight with bare hands.

SHAKUNI And I suppose some will also say that Uttara, who defeated all of us singlehanded, was actually Arjuna!

DRONA Do you have any doubt about it, lord of Gandhara? Could the drawing of Uttara's bow sound like a thunderclap in a cloudless sky? Could Uttara's arrows cover the sun and make it seem to set?

BHISHMA I tell you clearly, son of Gandhari. Indeed you know it. That bow-string resounded with the name marked on its arrows. Didn't you listen? It was drawn by Arjuna.

[Enter a Charioteer]

CHARIOTEER Victory to you, sir. Be ready to make peace.

BHISHMA Why?

CHARIOTEER Before your standard is struck by arrows it is better to make peace. Here is the arrow. Its feathers tell of someone's name.

BHISHMA Bring it here.

[Charioteer gives the arrow]

BHISHMA (*Takes and looks at it*) Lord of Gandhara, my child, my eyes are dim with age. Will you read what is written on this arrow?

SHAKUNI (*Takes and reads*) It is Arjuna's. (*Throws the arrow which falls at Drona's feet*)

DRONA (*Taking the arrow*) My child, this arrow was discharged by my pupil to salute Bhishma. Now it has fallen on the ground before my feet to salute me in turn.

SHAKUNI No, sir. Is this arrow a credible proof? It could have been shot by another warrior also named Arjuna. A proper proof must be produced, written by Uttara.

DURYODHANA And if he utters a falsehood to help the Pandavas get the kingdom? I will give half the kingdom only if I actually see Yudhishthira.

[Enter a Soldier]

SOLDIER Victory to the king. An envoy has come from the city of King Virata.

DURYODHANA Let him enter.

SOLDIER As the king commands. (*Exit*)

[Enter Uttara]

UTTARA The road was not long, and the horses had their head. But still my chariot was delayed on the way. The horses moved with difficulty as the ground was littered with elephants felled by Arjuna's arrows. (*Joining hands in salute*) My salutations to all the princes led by the preceptor and the grandfather.

ALL May you live long.

DRONA What does His Majesty the King Virata say?

UTTARA I have not been sent by His Majesty.

DRONA Then by whom have you been sent?

UTTARA By His Majesty Yudhishthira.

DRONA What does King Yudhishthira say?

UTTARA Listen. 'I have obtained Uttarā as a daughter-in-law. I now await you princes. Please advise if the wedding should be held here or there.'

SHAKUNI There! There!

DRONA So we have reached the conclusion. The five nights are not yet over. The fee agreed upon lawfully should now be given in accordance with the law.

DURYODHANA So be it. I give the kingdom to the Pandavas as earlier agreed. All men die, but if they uphold the truth, their words will live for ever.

DRONA O joy! All are happy. The families are united. May our lion king protect this earth entire.

[Exit all]

The Envoy
Dūta Vākyam

{3}

The Envoy

Dūta Vākyam

In the sequence of the *Mahābhārata* narrative this play comes after *The Middle One* and *Five Nights*. The setting of the first play was the Pandava princes in exile, in the forest, following the loss of their kingdom in a game of dice with their cousins and enemies, the Kauravas. In the second play, the exile comes to an end in the court of King Virata. *The Envoy* is set in the next phase when efforts are made, without success, to regain the kingdom by peaceful means. These phases correspond respectively to the third, fourth and fifth books of the epic, entitled Forest, Virata and Effort.

The period of Effort was marked by intense diplomatic activity prior to the great war. On the one hand, the Pandavas assembled their friends, particularly those with whom they had forged matrimonial alliances. These included the Panchala King Drupada, whose daughter Draupadi had earlier wed the five brothers; the Yadava chief Krishna, whose sister Subhadra had married Arjuna; and King Virata of Matsya, whose daughter had married the son of Arjuna and Subhadra at the end of the exile.

On the other hand, the Pandavas and the Kauravas exchanged a number of messages and emissaries. Their deliberations on the contents of such messages and the qualities of the emissary provide a considerable manual on the art of diplomacy, alongside other didactic or informative dissertations with which the epic abounds.

Eventually, Krishna himself went to the Kuru court to seek a peaceful solution. His mission is narrated in the epic at some length. In the Pandava camp there is a discussion, before his departure, on the stance he should take. The Kauravas discuss how he should be received: the elders feel he should be treated with honour; Duryodhana prefers to have him arrested. The actual mission lasts three days. On the final day, Krishna addresses the Kuru assembly. He and the elders try to persuade Duryodhana to divide the realm with the Pandavas. On his refusal, Krishna reproaches him and later suggests that he should be imprisoned in the interest of peace. Meanwhile, Duryodhana leaves the assembly and himself plans to capture Krishna. When he returns, Krishna manifests his cosmic form and then departs.

The story of Krishna's mission is presented in *The Envoy* in a single act. The picture depicting Draupadi's humiliation during the game of dice, exhibited by Duryodhana to belittle Krishna, has been invented by the dramatist to create an effect: it does not exist in the original epic. The appearance in personified form of Krishna's divine weapon, Sudarshana, is in the same category. In the original play Sudarshana is also accompanied briefly by some other divine weapons which have been excluded in this translation. Another feature of the play is the manner in which the Kaurava assembly's deliberations are acted out by Duryodhana in a long soliloquy.

The protagonists of the play are Krishna and Duryodhana. The latter is depicted as a proud and defiant figure, as in the other *Mahābhārata* plays of Bhasa. He appears as the actual king of the Kurus, even though his blind father is alive. The portrayal of Krishna is of particular interest. As in the epic, he is shown as both human and divine. The human aspect is more apparent in the first part of the play, particularly in the heated exchanges with Duryodhana. And even when the divine aspect is clearly manifested towards the end, there is still a human trace in the dialogue with Sudarshana.

Among the characters mentioned in the play, the Kuru nobles, Vaikarna and Varshadeva, are inventions of the dramatist. Jarasandha appears in the epic as the mighty king of Magadha who was friendly with the Kauravas and an enemy of Krishna.

He mounted so many military expeditions against Mathura, where Krishna originally ruled, that the latter was obliged to retreat and establish a new capital at Dwaraka on the western coast of India. Eventually, Jarasandha was killed by the Pandava prince Bhima. Kansa was Krishna's uncle and ruled over Mathura before he was killed by his nephew.

A complete understanding of the reference to Vichitravirya in the play requires some explanation of the practice of the *niyoga* in ancient India. Sons were considered essential for the performance of an individual's funeral rites which were necessary for assuring the welfare of the deceased in afterlife. They were also needed to ensure that the inheritance remained within the family. If a man could not beget a son due to some infirmity, or if he died without a male issue, it was admissible for his wife to bear a son *for him* from some other suitable person through the observance of the *niyoga* ritual; and such a son would be regarded as his own for religious and legal purposes.

The Kuru dynasty of Hastinapura had been perpetuated for two generations through the practice of *niyoga*. The King Vichitravirya died without any children though he had two wives. After his elder brother Bhishma had declined to cohabit with them as he had taken a vow of celibacy, the sage Vyasa was invited to father sons from them for Vichitravirya. The results were Dhritarashtra, the father of the Kauravas, and Pandu, the father of the Pandavas. Pandu also was prevented by a curse from having progeny. As such, with his consent, his wives bore for him the five Pandavas who were begotten of the gods.

The epilogue of the play is worthy of note as pointing to the geographical existence of a kingdom at the time. The same verse figures at the end of Bhasa's well-known play *Svapna Vāsavadattā* and also *Bālacharita*. Rajasimha, here translated as the lion-king, is also mentioned at the end of *Five Nights*. Whether this is the name or the title of a particular king remains a question for historians.

Cast in order of appearance

The Producer	*in the Prologue*
Chamberlain	*of the Kuru court, named Badarayana*
Duryodhana	*also called Suyodhana, king of the Kurus*
Krishna	*the god Narayana incarnate, also called Vishnu, Keshava*
Sudarshana	*the discus, the divine weapon of Vishnu personified*
Dhritarashtra	*the blind old king, father of Duryodhana*

Other characters mentioned in the play

Vaikarna	*a Kuru noble*
Varshadeva	*a Kuru noble*
Preceptor	*Dronacharya, teacher of the Kauravas and the Pandavas*
Grandfather	*Bhishma, elder of the Kuru clan, also called son of Ganga*
Uncle	*Shakuni, prince of Gandhara, brother of Gandhari, Duryodhana's mother*
Karna	*a famous warrior, friend of Duryodhana*
Draupadi	*wife of the Pandava brothers, Yudhishthira, Bhima, Arjuna, Nakula and Sahdeva, the cousins of Duryodhana*
Duhshasana, Durmarshana, Durmukha, Durbuddhi, Dushteshvara	*brothers of Duryodhana*
Vichitravirya	*father of Dhritarashtra, husband of Ambika*

Prologue

[After the benediction, enter the Producer]

PRODUCER May the feet of Vishnu protect you; the feet with slender rosy nails, which gladden all the worlds and which sent the demon Namuchi hurtling through the sky.

And now, distinguished spectators, I have to announce that—but what is that? There seems to be a sound just as I was about to start. Well, let me see.

[Voices off stage]

VOICES Attention! Attention, you guards. King Duryodhana has commanded . . .

PRODUCER Ah, I see. Discord having arisen between the sons of Dhritarashtra and the sons of Pandu, an attendant is preparing the council chamber at Duryodhana's command.

[Exit]

[END OF PROLOGUE]

ACT I

[Enter a Chamberlain]

CHAMBERLAIN Attention! Attention, you guards. King Duryodhana has commanded that all the princes be summoned as he wishes to consult with them today. But, oh, there is King Duryodhana himself coming this way. There, with the royal parasol and flywhisk. He wears a white silk mantle on his dark, youthful body, perfumed and gleaming with jewels. He is splendid, like the full moon among the stars.

[Enter Duryodhana, as described]

DURYODHANA The anger in my heart has suddenly given way to joy at the thought that the festival of war is at hand. Now my only wish is to tear out the tusks of the finest elephants in the Pandava army.

CHAMBERLAIN Victory to the great king. All the princes have been assembled as commanded by Your Majesty.

DURYODHANA Well done. You may go inside.

CHAMBERLAIN As Your Majesty commands. (*Exit*)

DURYODHANA My lords Vaikarna and Varshadeva, I have a force of eleven armies. Tell me, who is fit to be its Commander-in-Chief? What did you say? It is an important matter. It should be decided after consultations. Quite so. Then come, let us go into the council chamber.

Greetings, preceptor. Please come into the council chamber, sir. Greetings, grandfather, please come into the council chamber. Uncle, greetings. Please enter the council chamber. Enter, lords Vaikarna and Varshadeva. Enter freely, all you warriors. Comrade Karna, let us go in. (*Entering*) Preceptor, here is the tortoise throne. Please be seated. Grandfather, please take your seat on the lion throne. Uncle, this is the leather throne. Please take a seat. Lords Vaikarna and Varshadeva, please take a seat. Please be seated all you warriors. What? The king is not seated? What devotion! Well, I will sit down. Friend Karna, please sit also. (*Sitting down*) Lords Vaikarna and Varshadeva, I have a force of eleven armies. Tell me, who should be its Commander-in-Chief? What did you say? Let the prince of Gandhara speak. Very well. Let my uncle speak. What did uncle say? Who else can be the Commander-in-Chief when the son of Ganga is there? Well spoken, uncle. Very well, so be it. Grandfather, that is also our wish. Let the hearts of their leaders sink even as the son of Ganga is anointed to the roars of acclaim of our army.

[Enter the Chamberlain]

CHAMBERLAIN Victory to Your Majesty. Krishna, the best of men, has come from the Pandava camp as an envoy.

DURYODHANA Don't speak like that, Badarayana! Is that servant of Kansa your best of men? Is that herder of cows your best of men? Is that your best of men who was deprived by Jarasandha of his lands and reputation? It this the way the king's servant should behave? With such insolent words? You . . . .

CHAMBERLAIN Have mercy, great king. I forgot he proper conduct in my confusion. (*Falls at his feet*)

DURYODHANA Confusion? Ah well, people do get confused. You may get up.

CHAMBERLAIN Oh, thank you, Your Majesty.

DURYODHANA It is all right. Now, who is this envoy who has arrived?

CHAMBERLAIN The envoy who has come is one Keshava.

DURYODHANA Keshava! That's better. That's the proper conduct. O you princes, what will be proper for this Keshava who has come as an envoy? What did you say? He should be received with honours? That doesn't appeal to me. I see merit in arresting him. If Keshava is arrested the Pandavas would have lost their eyes. And, with the Pandavas deprived of direction and advice, the whole earth will be mine, without a rival.

Moreover, if anyone gets up to receive Keshava, he will be fined twelve gold coins by me. So, don't forget that, gentlemen. Now, what should be the reason for my not getting up? Ah, that's it. Badarayana! Bring me that painting which shows Draupadi being dragged by her hair and her garments. (*Aside*) I will look at it and not get up for Keshava.

CHAMBERLAIN As Your Majesty commands. (*Exits and re-enters*) Victory to the great king. Here is that painting.

DURYODHANA Spread it out before me.

CHAMBERLAIN As Your Majesty commands. (*Spreads it out*)

DURYODHANA This is a picture worth seeing. Here is Duhshasana, holding Draupadi by the hair. Here is Draupadi, seized by Duhshasana and wide-eyed with terror. She looks like a digit of the moon in eclipse.

And here is that wretch Bhima, sizing up the pillars of the hall as he angrily watches Draupadi being humiliated before all the princes. Here is Yudhishthira, quietening Bhima with sidelong looks. He is the righteous and truthful one, stupefied by the game of dice.

And here now is Arjuna, eyes filled with rage, lips trembling. He has such contempt for his enemies. He slowly draws the string of his bow, as if he would destroy them all. But Yudhishthira stops him.

And here are Nakula and Sahadeva, faces flushed, swords in hand, ready to fight. Recklessly they attack my brother, like two calves against a tiger. But Yudhishthira restrains them. And here is the prince of Gandhara, laughing and casting the dice, as he gazes at the weeping Draupadi from his couch. And Grandfather and the preceptor stand there, covering their heads with their mantles, ashamed to see her. What rich colours! What fine expressions! How perfect a composition! This picture is really well done. I like it. Who is there?

CHAMBERLAIN Victory to the great king.

DURYODHANA Badarayana, bring in that envoy who is so proud just because he rides on a bird.

CHAMBERLAIN As Your Majesty commands. (*Exit*)

DURYODHANA Well, Karna my friend. The crafty Krishna has come here on a mission, like a servant of the Pandavas. Let us get ready to hear the soft feminine words of Yudhishthira.

[Enter Krishna with the Chamberlain]

KRISHNA It is not fitting to come as an envoy to the proud Suyodhana who grasps at even the unsaid word. But I am here today at the request of Yudhishthira and out of true friendship for Arjuna. The Kuru clan is going to be destroyed in the fire of Bhima's anger, fanned by Arjuna's arrows and the disgrace of Draupadi.

Well, here is Suyodhana's camp. The royal quarters look like paradise: the arsenals are full of weapons; the horses neigh and the elephants trumpet. But none of this opulence can survive war among kinsmen. This villain Suyodhana has no feelings for his kin. He speaks ill, dislikes virtues and is not going to do what he should, even on seeing me.

Well, Badarayana, should one go in?

CHAMBERLAIN Of course, of course. Please enter, Krishna.

KRISHNA (*Entering*) What is this? All the warriors seem confused on seeing me. Sit at ease, gentlemen. There is no need for any agitation.

DURYODHANA What is this? All the warriors seem confused on seeing Krishna. Enough of this. Please remember the fine which has been ordained. I give the orders here.

KRISHNA O Suyodhana, how are you?

DURYODHANA (*Falling down from his seat, aside*) It is clear that Krishna has arrived. I had made up my mind to keep sitting, but his power moved me from my seat. This envoy is a cunning magician. (*Aloud*) Here is a seat, ambassador, please be seated.

KRISHNA Preceptor, take a seat. Bhishma and the princes, please sit as you wish. We will also sit. (*Sits down*) Oh, what a nice painting. But no! It depicts Draupadi being dragged by the hair! This childish Suyodhana thinks it brave to humiliate his kinsmen. Otherwise, who in this world would display his own faults in an assembly. O take away this painting.

DURYODHANA Badarayana! Take that picture away.

CHAMBERLAIN As Your Majesty commands. (*Removes picture*)

DURYODHANA Well, ambassador, how are my brothers, the son of Dharma, Bhima the son of the wind god, Arjuna the son of the king of gods and the modest sons of the twin gods. Are they and their people well?

KRISHNA Worthily spoken. O son of Gandhari, indeed they are all well. And they have also enquired about your welfare and that of your kingdom. Yudhishthira and his brothers also want to inform you that they have suffered many sorrows. The time has now come. So let the inheritance be divided, and the due share given to them.

DURYODHANA What inheritance? My uncle committed a crime while hunting in the forest. The sage cursed him and he became impotent with his wives. He had no progeny. How can a patrimony go to the sons of others?

KRISHNA Since you know history, sir, let me also ask you. Vichitravirya was addicted to pleasures and died of the wasting sickness. Your father Dhritarashtra was born to Ambika from Vyasa. Then how did he succeed to the kingdom? No, no, sir. By this way of mutual confrontation the Kuru clan may soon become just a name. It is better to give up anger and accept what Yudhishthira and the others have lovingly requested.

DURYODHANA Mister ambassador, you do not understand the ways of kings. One does not beg for a kingdom, nor give it as charity. Kingdoms are won by princes with stout hearts who defeat their enemies. If the Pandavas desire dominion let them act boldly. Otherwise let them enter a hermitage and live there with peace-minded monks.

KRISHNA O that is enough of harsh words for your kinsmen, Suyodhana. Sovereignty is attained by the accumulated merit of past good deeds. All is lost by cheating relatives and well-wishers.

DURYODHANA You had no pity for King Kansa, the brother-in-law of your own father. Why should we have it for those who have always harmed us?

KRISHNA That was not my fault. He invited death by imprisoning his old father and making my mother suffer the loss of successive sons.

DURYODHANA Kansa was wholly betrayed by you. There is no need for self-praise. It was not a brave deed. And where was your bravery when you fled, terrified, from the king of Magadha who was enraged at his son-in-law's murder?

KRISHNA Suyodhana, the wise man's bravery accords with the time, the place and the situation. But, leave aside this mutual pleasantry and come to my business. Have love for your brothers. Forget their faults. Good relations with kinsmen have merit in both this and the next world.

DURYODHANA How can there be kinship between mortal men and the sons of gods? You repeat the same old tale. It is enough. Put an end to it.

KRISHNA (*Aside*) he does not change his attitude by conciliation. Well, I must try him with strong words. (*Aloud*) Suyodhana, don't you know the might and power of Arjuna?

DURYODHANA I don't.

KRISHNA Listen. He gave satisfaction in battle to Lord Shiva disguised as a hunter. With his arrows he held off the downpour of rain over the burning Khandava forests. He destroyed the armoured demons as if in sport. He defeated Bhishma and the rest singlehanded at the city of King Virata.

Another thing you yourself witnessed. On your visit to the cattle farm, when Chitrasena carried you off screaming in the sky, Arjuna released you. In short, son of Dhritarashtra, kindly give half the kingdom as I have suggested. Otherwise the Pandavas will seize it right up to the sea.

DURYODHANA What did you say? The Pandavas will seize it? Let the wind-god in the shape of Bhima attack us in battle. Let the king of gods himself strike us in the person of Arjuna. Not a blade of grass will I give of this kingdom, held and protected by my forefathers. Not for all your harsh words, ambassador.

KRISHNA You worthless blot on the house of Kuru! Are we discussing blades of grass!

DURYODHANA Cowherd! Grass is indeed the thing for you, sir. Having killed an innocent woman, and horses and bulls and wrestlers, you shamelessly want to speak with respectable people!

KRISHNA Suyodhana, are you chiding me?

DURYODHANA You are not worthy of being spoken with. I bear the royal white umbrella. My head is anointed with water from the hands of high priests. You are no better than a follower of my vassal kings, I do not speak with the likes of you. I tell them.

KRISHNA Indeed, Suyodhana does not speak with me. You villain! You evil-eyed crow! You snake! The Kuru clan will soon be destroyed because of you. I leave now, O you princes.

DURYODHANA How can Krishna leave? He has transgressed the proper conduct of envoys. Duhshasana! Durmarshana! Durmukha! Durbuddhi! Dushteshvara! Arrest him! What? You cannot? Duhshasana! You are not able? This Krishna has no strength or power. He is at fault by his own mouth in front of princes. He should be arrested immediately. But you cannot! Uncle, arrest Krishna! What? He turns his face and falls! Very well, I will arrest him myself. (*Advances*)

KRISHNA Suyodhana wants to arrest me! Very well. Let me see if he can. (*Assumes the Universal Form*)

DURYODHANA Envoy, today you are going to be arrested by me in front of all these princes. Despite your pride. Even though you make magic black or white. Even though you use difficult divine weapons. Just wait. But how has Krishna disappeared? Ah, here he is. How small he seems. Just wait. How has he disappeared again? Ah, here he is. How large he seems. How has he disappeared once more? Here he is. But there are Krishnas everywhere in the council chamber. What should I do now? Very well. O you princes, each one of you arrest one Krishna. What? The princes are falling down, bound with their own cords. Well done, magician, well done! The Pandavas shall see you with sighs and tearful eyes, when you are carried to their camp, with your limbs pierced by my arrows. (*Exit*)

KRISHNA Very well. I will myself complete this work for the Pandavas. Come here, O Sudarshana!

[Enter Sudarshana, the divine discus]

SUDARSHANA Here I am. Hearing the lord's voice, and with his grace, I have sped here through the clouds. At whom is the lotus-eyed lord angered? On whose head should I appear today?

But, where is the Lord Narayana, the protector of the world, the destroyer of enemies, the splendid one of many forms, the first, the un-manifest and immeasurable soul? (*Looking around*) Ah, there is the lord, in the role of an envoy at the gate of Hastinapura. Water! Where is the ritual water? Some water, O lady Ganga of the sky! Ah, it flows.

(*Performs ablution, and approaches*) Victory to Lord Narayana! (*Makes salutation*).

KRISHNA Sudarshana! Be matchless in power.

SUDARSHANA I thank you.

KRISHNA Fortunately you have arrived just in time, sir.

SUDARSHANA Just in time? Command me, lord, command me. Shall I overturn the mountains? Shall I convulse the sea? Shall I pluck out the stars? O God, by your grace there is nothing impossible for me.

KRISHNA Come here, Sudarshana. And you, rash Suyodhana, whether you flee to mountain caves, or to the salty sea, or to the windswept, star-crossed sky, today my swift-propelled discus will be the discus of your death.

SUDARSHANA Suyodhana, you wretch! (*Thinking further*) Mercy! Mercy, Lord Narayana. You have come upon this earth to ease its burdens. In this way, the effort would be wasted, O God!

KRISHNA Sudarshana! The proper conduct was overlooked by me in anger. Return to your abode.

SUDARSHANA As the Lord Narayana commands. How can he be called a cowherd? He who transcended the three worlds in three strides? All should seek refuge in him. I go . . . I will return to my dear recess in Mount Meru.

KRISHNA I too will leave for the camp of the Pandavas.

[Voice off stage]

VOICE No, no, he must not leave.

KRISHNA That sounds like the old king. I am here, O king.

[Enter Dhritarashtra]

DHRITARASHTRA Where is the Lord Narayana? Where is the Pandavas' benefactor, the beloved of the virtuous, the delight of Devaki. O Ruler of the three worlds, my son offended you. Now my head is placed at your feet.

KRISHNA Oh dear! Your Majesty prostrates! Arise, arise.

DHRITARASHTRA I thank you, lord. Please accept this ritual water of welcome.

KRISHNA I accept it all. What can I offer you in return?

DHRITARASHTRA If the lord is pleased, what else can I wish for?

KRISHNA Go, sir, till we meet again.

DHRITARASHTRA As the Lord Narayana commands. (*Exit*)

Epilogue

May the Lion King
lead us on this land adorned
by the Himalayas and the Vindhyas,
and stretched from sea to sea
in single sovereignty.

The Message
Dūta Ghatotkacham

{4}

The Message

Dūta Ghatotkacham

The setting of this play is based on the seventh book of the epic, when the Mahābhārata war is raging at its fiercest. The play describes a visit by the Pandava partisan, Ghatotkacha, to the Kaurava camp with a message of dire warning from Krishna. No such visit or message exists in the original epic, and the play is another example of the dramatist's creative imagination.

The rules of chivalry were largely observed on all sides during the first ten days of the war, while the patriarch Bhishma commanded the Kaurava armies. They were contravened in the fall of Bhishma, when Arjuna attacked him from the cover of a eunuch, knowing that the old warrior would not bear arms against one who was not a man. Thereafter the fighting became more cruel and treacherous. A dramatic instance of this was the death of Abhimanyu.

Five Nights had ended with Abhimanyu's wedding. He was Arjuna's son, Krishna's nephew, and the heir of the Pandavas. After his father had been lured away into a distant battle with an auxiliary force, this youth was trapped alone within the *chakravyūha* or wheel formation of the Kaurava army. There he was surrounded by seven leading enemy warriors, and unfairly slain, while Jayadratha, husband of Duryodhana's sister Duhshala, blocked the way for Pandava rescue efforts.

Arjuna, deeply grieved, swore an oath that he would kill Jayadratha before the sun set on the following day, or himself commit suicide. Krishna helped him with a divine intervention in fulfilling his vow. This is the background of the present play.

Ghatotkacha is earlier encountered in *The Middle One*. He is the son of Arjuna's brother Bhima and the demoness Hidimba. Using the magic powers of demons he later wreaks havoc on the Kaurava armies, until he is stopped by Karna with an infallible weapon the latter has been saving for use against Arjuna. While Ghatotkacha is a minor figure in the *Mahābhārata*, he must have attracted sufficient popular interest at some stage to feature in these two plays. It is interesting to note in this context that the founder of the historical Gupta dynasty of North India bore the name Ghatotkacha. The character also has a comparatively more prominent place in the Javanese version of the epic, and the present writer has witnessed in Indonesia a wayang drama entitled 'Ghatotkacha in Love'.

Abhimanyu is described in the play as the grandson of Indra, the king of the gods. This is a reference to Arjuna being the natural son of Indra. The prowess of Arjuna as the greatest warrior of the time is mentioned in terms of his earlier adventures during which he defeated various demons, engaged the great god Shiva, disguised as a hunter, in single combat, and covered the burning Khandava forest with a net of arrows to prevent the fire being quenched by rain.

Arjuna's rival is the hero of the next play, *Karna's Burden*. There is a certain overlap between the references to Karna in that play and in the present one. For example, his being tricked by Indra into giving away his armour is mentioned in *The Message* as already having happened, but depicted only in the next play.

Duryodhana's father, the blind king Dhritarashtra, has a fleeting appearance at the end of *The Envoy*. Here his character is developed at greater length, and his wife also makes an appearance.

He is portrayed as a worried old man in considerable awe of Krishna who is referred to in terms both human and divine.

This play comes under the Sanskrit literary classification *anka*, a one-act piece evoking the heroic and the compassionate flavours. A note is struck at its beginning with the recollection of the deaths of the eldest and the youngest of the warriors in the conflict, Bhishma and Abhimanyu. Pathos and grief are evoked in the first part around the figure of the blind king. These give way to heroic exchanges with the entry of the demon messenger, ending with a note of terror. The opening benediction is notable for its reference to the dramatist's craft, the terminology of which is used to describe the divine supervision of the universe. The Sanskrit terms used are those for the prologue, main plot and epilogue of a theatrical performance, and the deity is invoked as the *sutradhāra* or director of the cosmic drama.

Cast in order of appearance

The Producer	*in the Prologue*
A Soldier	*of the Kauravas, named Jayatrata*
Dhritarashtra	*the blind old king, father of Duryodhana and other Kauravas, and uncle of the Pandavas*
Gandhari	*wife of Dhritarashtra*
Duhshala	*daughter of Dhritarashtra*
An Attendant	*of Gandhari*
Duryodhana	*chief of the Kauravas*
Duhshasana	*brother of Duryodhana*
Shakuni	*brother of Gandhari*
Ghatotkacha	*son of the demoness Hidimba by the Pandava prince Bhima.*

Other characters mentioned in the play

Arjuna	*Pandava prince, natural son of Indra*
Krishna	*divine charioteer of Arjuna*
Abhimanyu	*Arjuna's son, and Krishna's nephew*
Jayadratha	*Kaurava warrior, husband of Duhshala*
Uttarā	*wife of Abhimanyu*
Bhishma	*Kaurava patriarch*
Karna	*Kaurava warrior*
Samshaptaka	*a tribe allied with the Kauravas in their war against the Pandavas, their cousins*
Indra	*king of the gods*

Prologue

[After the benediction, enter the Producer]

PRODUCER May Narayana protect you all. He, who guides the gods, and directs the ceaseless drama of this universe from its opening to the final curtain. He, who is the one well-wisher of the three worlds. (*Walks about*) And now, distinguished spectators, I have to announce that—but what is that? There seems to be a sound just as I was about to start. Well, let me see.

[Voices off stage]

VOICE Ho there! Let it be known! Let it be known . . .

PRODUCER Ah, I see. When Arjuna and Krishna were challenged by the Samshaptaka army, the sons of Dhritarashtra, enraged at the fall of Bhishma, surrounded and slew the boy Abhimanyu. Now those princes are returning to their camps, wounded by Abhimanyu's arrows and fearful of Arjuna's counter-attack.

[Exit]

[END OF PROLOGUE]

ACT I

[Enter a Soldier]

SOLDIER Ho there! Let it be known to King Dhritarashtra, the far-sighted, the wise, the father of a hundred sons, that the boy Abhimanyu performed like Arjuna in the battlefield. He assailed the royal army and destroyed numerous chariots, elephants, horses and soldiers. But many princes came upon him from all directions and despatched him to the embrace of his grandfather in heaven.

[Enter Dhritarashtra, Gandhari, Duhshala and an Attendant]

DHRITARASHTRA O what is this? Who pollutes my ears? Who speaks ill, thinking I will like it? Who dares to announce the extinction of our line stained with the murder of our child?

GANDHARI Your Majesty, it seems to me that this family feud will destroy our children.

DHRITARASHTRA It is obvious, Gandhari.

GANDHARI Why, Your Majesty?

DHRITARASHTRA Gandhari, listen. Arjuna and Krishna will be incensed at the death of Abhimanyu. Today, with Krishna wielding the whip and the reins, Arjuna will destroy everyone with his terrible bow. Only then will there be peace.

GANDHARI O Abhimanyu, my child! Where have you gone so playfully, grandson, when fate has brought this terrible civil war upon us?

DUHSHALA The man who has caused our daughter-in-law Uttarā to be widowed today has made it certain that his women too will become widows.

DHRITARASHTRA Now who is the bearer of this news?

SOLDIER Your Majesty, it is I.

DHRITARASHTRA Who are you, sir?

SOLDIER I am Jayatrata, Your Majesty.

DHRITARASHTRA Jayatrata, who killed Abhimanyu? Who finds living disagreeable? Who wants to become fuel for the fire of the Pandavas?

SOLDIER Your Majesty, many warriors killed prince Abhimanyu together. But Jayadratha was the cause.

DHRITARASHTRA Alas, that Jayadratha was the cause!

SOLDIER How is that, Your Majesty?

DHRITARASHTRA Alas! Jayadratha is as good as dead.

[Duhshala begins to weep on hearing this]

DHRITARASHTRA Who is that weeping?

ATTENDANT It is the princess Duhshala, Your Majesty.

DHRITARASHTRA Do not weep, my child. Your husband obviously does not care for the marital state. He has himself made his person the target of Arjuna's arrows.

DUHSHALA Then give me permission, father. I too will go to Uttarā.

DHRITARASHTRA My child! What are you saying?

DUHSHALA And I will tell her, father, that the weeds she wears today, I too will wear tomorrow.

GANDHARI Daughter, don't speak such inauspicious words. Your husband is very much alive.

DUHSHALA Do I have such good fortune, mother? Who can expect to live if he has angered Arjuna, assisted by Krishna?

DHRITARASHTRA Poor Duhshala speaks the truth. Abhimanyu was brought up in the arms of Krishna. Love for him intoxicated Balarama. He was the apple of the Pandava eye. They are powerful like the gods. Who in this world can expect to live long after killing him?

Jayatrata! What did Arjuna do after seeing his son in that condition?

SOLDIER It did not happen in front of Arjuna, Your Majesty.

DHRITARASHTRA What? Arjuna was not there?

SOLDIER What else.

DHRITARASHTRA What did happen?

SOLDIER Listen. When Arjuna, assisted by Krishna, was challenged by the Samshaptaka army, Prince Abhimanyu entered the battle, youthfully heedless of danger.

DHRITARASHTRA Alas! The circumstances were suited to his death. Who could have entered the lion's den if the lion had been there. And now, what are the Pandavas doing?

SOLDIER Your Majesty, they will not place his body on the funeral pyre till Arjuna has seen it. Meanwhile they are determining the names of the princes who had struck him.

DHRITARASHTRA Then come, Gandhari, let us also go to the bank of the Ganga.

GANDHARI Indeed, Your Majesty, we will all bathe there.

DHRITARASHTRA Today itself, Gandhari, I will offer the funeral water for your sons. They are going to perish because of my mistakes. Even though I cannot stop their campaign with this water offering.

[Enter Duryodhana, Duhshasana and Shakuni]

DURYODHANA Well, Duhshasana, with the death of Abhimanyu our cause has become stronger. We have won a victory. The enemy is repulsed and shaken. Krishna's pride is shattered. Today I have obtained both success and recognition.

DUHSHASANA Certainly. Jayadratha's attack on the enemy stopped the Pandavas. Our grief at Bishma's fall in battle was matched today when Abhimanyu, the second Arjuna, fell to a hundred arrows. His fall is like a sharp arrow of grief in the heart of the Pandavas.

SHAKUNI Jayadratha performed impossible feats in battle today. He deprived the Pandavas perforce of both their son and their reputation.

DURYODHANA This way, uncle. Duhshasana, this way. We will greet our respected father.

SHAKUNI No, Duryodhana, not so. This fight in the family does not please him at all. He blames us because of his love for the Pandavas. It will be best to go to him with happy faces once the war is won and over.

DURYODHANA No, uncle. Whatever may happen we will greet our respected father.

OTHER TWO Very well.

[All walk around]

DURYODHANA Father, Duryodhana greets you.

DUHSHASANA Father, Duhshasana greets you.

SHAKUNI Shakuni greets you.

ALL Aren't you going to bless us?

DHRITARASHTRA What blessing, son? What is the use of blessings for those who do not care for their own lives? When that boy, the beloved of Krishna and Arjuna, has been slain?

DURYODHANA Father, why this agitation?

DHRITARASHTRA Why this agitation? In this family of a hundred sons there is only one daughter, the most beloved of all. And she is going to be widowed, thanks to her brothers.

DURYODHANA Why, father, what has Jayadratha done?

DHRITARASHTRA That clever son-in-law of mine stopped the Pandavas.

DURYODHANA He stopped them? But there were many others also.

DHRITARASHTRA O why did not their arms fall off, when they struck down that boy so pitilessly. So many against one child.

DURYODHANA Father! His prowess was hardly that of a child. And why would our arms fall off? Did their arms fall off when they brought Bhishma down by deceit?

DHRITARASHTRA My son, can the fall of Bhishma and the killing of Abhimanyu be compared?

DURYODHANA Why not, father?

DHRITARASHTRA Listen, my son. Bhishma fell by his own choice and according to his own advice. He had satisfied himself. This was just a boy. A budding flower, Arjuna's first, was cut down. He would have been the future lord of the Kurus.

DUHSHASANA Father, he was not a child, Abhimanyu. . . .

DHRITARASHTRA Is that Duhshasana speaking?

DUHSHASANA Who else? We all watched and fought as he wielded the bow which was smouldering with use. He showered all the princes with his arrows as the sun does with its rays.

DHRITARASHTRA O if a single lad could do all this, what won't the grief-stricken Arjuna do to us?

DURYODHANA What will he do?

DHRITARASHTRA You will see what he does. If you survive to see it.

DURYODHANA So, what is Arjuna, father?

DHRITARASHTRA Don't you know him, my son?

DURYODHANA I don't, father.

DHRITARASHTRA Then I don't either. But there are many who are aware of Arjuna's might. Ask them.

DURYODHANA Father, who are these connoisseurs of Arjuna's might whom I should ask?

DHRITARASHTRA My son, ask the king of the gods to whom Arjuna presented the armoured demons as a trophy. Ask the great god, disguised as a hunter, whom Arjuna held to a draw in armed combat. Ask the god of fire whom Arjuna pleased with the offering of the Khandava forest with all its serpents. Or ask Chitrangada and his army, who had captured you till Arjuna secured your release.

DURYODHANA Even if Arjuna is so mighty, aren't there equal warriors in our army?

DHRITARASHTRA Who are they, my son?

DURYODHANA Obviously there is Karna.

DHRITARASHTRA Poor Karna? That is ridiculous.

DURYODHANA Why?

DHRITARASHTRA He is only half a warrior. He is too careless and kind. He let Indra take away his armour. The weapons he obtained by subterfuge will not work. He would be a match for Arjuna only if the fire-god, the great god and the king of the gods were to give him their weapons.

SHAKUNI You excel in slighting us, sir.

DHRITARASHTRA Is that Shakuni who speaks? And you, Shakuni, excel in gambling. What you have always done is to fan the flames of enmity in this family so that they will not subside even among the children.

DURYODHANA O what is that sudden sound? It shakes the earth and sets the sky aflame, like a falling meteor.

DHRITARASHTRA I think those are Indra's tears of anguish which fall like meteors from heaven. He has clearly seen his grandson killed.

DURYODHANA Jayatrata, go to the Pandava camp and find out who has caused this noise with a tumult of conch-shells, drumbeats and roars.

SOLDIER As you command. (*Exit and re-enters*) Victory to Your Majesty. Arjuna returned from the battle with the Samshaptaka army. He took his dead son in his arms and drenched him with tears. Incited by Krishna, he has made a vow.

DURYODHANA What? What?

SOLDIER Arjuna's vow heartened the angry princes assembled there. They bestride the earth like mountains. Arjuna's valour pleases them no end. Anticipating victory, they suddenly roared with joy. And the earth trembled for a moment like a girl.

DHRITARASHTRA The earth trembled at his vow alone! All the three worlds will doubtless shake when he grasps his bow.

DURYODHANA Jayatrata, what has he vowed?

SOLDIER Those who killed my son, and those who were pleased at his death, them I will destroy before the sun sets tomorrow.

DURYODHANA And if the vow is not fulfilled? What will be the penalty?

SOLDIER He will mount the funeral pyre with his bow.

DURYODHANA Uncle! He will mount the funeral pyre! Duhshasana! He will mount the pyre! We must make arrangements so that his vow is not fulfilled.

DHRITARASHTRA What will you do, son?

DURYODHANA Indeed, I will hide Jayadratha within our armies. With the advice of Drona I will arrange an impenetrable army formation to frustrate their intentions, so that they may enter the fire together with their war elephants and warriors.

DHRITARASHTRA Krishna is the eyes of Arjuna. His arrows will follow Jayadratha whether he burrows inside the earth or mounts into the heavens.

SOLDIER If anyone else were to speak thus to our stern and imperious lord he would not live beyond that moment.

[Enter Ghatotkacha]

GHATOTKACHA The death of Abhimanyu and the command of Krishna have brought me here today, like an elephant goaded towards the sacrificial offering. I wish to see the evil-hearted enemy. (*Looking down*) This must be the gate of his assembly hall. So I will get down. (*Getting down*) I will introduce myself. Ho! I am Ghatotkacha, son of Hidimba. I have come with a message from Krishna. I wish to see the elders who have now become enemies because of their own misconduct.

DURYODHANA Come! Come! Enter the enemy's hall. Here am I, Duryodhana. Great is my curiosity. Give me Krishna's message without any fear.

GHATOTKACHA (*Entering*) Oh, that is His Majesty Dhritarashtra, progenitor of a hundred wicked sons. What a deep and delicate appearance. It is marvellous. He is old, but with a face unlined and shoulders smooth and muscular. He is revered as a father a hundred times over. I think the gods were fearful for heaven's security, so they made him blind from birth.
(*Approaching*) Grandsire! I, Ghatotkacha greet . . . (*Interrupting himself*) No, no, that is not in order. First, the greetings from my elders, Yudhishthira and the others. Only then my own.

DHRITARASHTRA Come, my child. You are grieved at your brother's death. It is my grief also. This you cannot understand. How wretched I am because of the faults of my son.

GHATOTKACHA Your Majesty is gracious indeed. You are the fountain of graces, grandsire. For you the discus-wielding lord Krishna says . . .

DHRITARASHTRA (*Rising up from his seat*) What has the discus-wielding lord commanded?

GHATOTKACHA No, no, sir. You must hear Krishna's message seated on your throne.

DHRITARASHTRA As he commands. (*Sits down*)

GHATOTKACHA Listen, grandsire. 'Alas, my child Abhimanyu! Alas, my child, lamp of the house of Kuru! Alas, my child, blossom of the clan of Yadu! Forsaking your mother, your uncle and even me you have gone to heaven to your grandfather.' Such is the condition of Arjuna, grandsire, because of the loss of but one son. What then will be yours, sir? Therefore, withdraw your army quickly, so that the fire ignited by grief for your sons does not consume your life. This is the message.

DHRITARASHTRA Krishna has said this with deliberate anger. I see that Arjuna is determined to destroy all our warriors.

ALL Oh, what a ridiculous statement.

GHATOTKACHA What is ridiculous about it?

DURYODHANA What is ridiculous? This Krishna, this mischief-maker, must be communing with the gods to think that Arjuna alone can destroy an assembly of kings.

GHATOTKACHA I deliver Krishna's message, and you laugh? Perhaps it is better to tell you about the deeds of Arjuna. And you must also hear Krishna's message.

DUHSHASANA Stop! You insult us. Can the message of anyone else be heard in the presence of a king at whose command alone other princes rule the earth?

GHATOTKACHA What did you say? Is Krishna less than a king, Duhshasana? He who liberated captive kings in the past? He who received ceremonial water from Bhishma's hands while other kings watched. He on whom royal glory dotes? He is a king among kings.

DURYODHANA Enough of this argument, Duhshasana. It does not matter if he is strong or weak, a king or not a king. Sir, what does your master say?

GHATOTKACHA That is right. He is the master, the discus-wielding lord of the three worlds.

Specially, our master. Remember also that when the angry Arjuna releases his weapons at the head of battle, the destruction of your warriors is as good as accomplished. There will be a hundred princes fewer on this earth.

SHAKUNI If words alone could kill warriors and conquer the earth, then we should consider it done already.

GHATOTKACHA Is that Shakuni speaking? Put away the dice, Shakuni. Make arrows fit for battle out of the gaming board. This is not a game of stealing women or kingdoms. Here it is played with sharp arrows and the stake is life.

DURYODHANA Calm yourself. You break the bounds of decorum. You use harsh and abusive language. You talk tall without any consideration. If your arrogance is uncivilized like your mother's family, we also can be terrible like demons.

GHATOTKACHA Heaven forbid! You are even more cruel than demons. They at least do not burn their sleeping bretheren in a house of lac. They do not lay hands on their brother's wife. They do not remember to kill children in battle. Demons may be terrifying in appearance and conduct, but they are not merciless.

DURYODHANA You are an envoy, sir. You have not come here for battle. So take your message and go. We do not kill envoys.

GHATOTKACHA (*Angrily*) Are you trying to demean me by calling me an envoy? No, sir. I am not an envoy. Enough of this. Strike me, if you can. I am not defenceless like Abhimanyu with his bowstring cut off. This is what I have waited for since youth. Here stands Ghatotkacha, with teeth clenched and fists raised. Let anyone come up who wishes to be sent to hell.

DHRITARASHTRA Ghatotkacha, my grandchild, please forgive us. Pay attention to my words.

GHATOTKACHA All right. If the grandsire says I am an envoy, I accept. But even so I cannot control my anger. What is the request?

DURYODHANA Whose request? Just convey my words. They are: too much talk is useless. We cannot be defeated by your abuse. Angry words will get you nowhere. Say what you have to, in battle. I will come there with my princes while you stand with the Pandavas. And there, Krishna, I will give you my reply with arrows.

GHATOTKACHA I go, grandsire.

DHRITARASHTRA Go, grandson, go.

GHATOTKACHA Listen to Krishna's final message, you princes. Do all your good deeds. Look after your families. Enjoy your hearts' desires. For death, in the guise of Arjuna, will come to you at sunrise.

[Exit all]

Karna's Burden

Karnabhāram

{5}

Karna's Burden

Karnabhāram

This play is set in the penultimate phase of the Mahābhārata war. Its predecessor, *The Message*, which presented the battle as still equal, had ended with a warning of the destruction facing the Kaurava side. The present composition indicates that the beginning of the end has already commenced. The Kaurava champion, Karna, goes forth to fight with a premonition of doom. As he seeks combat with his rival, Arjuna, he seems to know that his time has come. The audience, familiar with the epic, know this already, and the dramatist, aware of their foreknowledge, has devised the plot to convey a mood of inevitability. The play ends before it reaches a climax. Its type is again the *anka*, combining the flavours of heroism and pathos.

Karna is the tragic hero of the *Mahābhārata*. He sought high recognition for his abilities, but was unfairly frustrated at every step. Though these frustrations warped his character to some extent, its essential nobility remained intact. Presented in detail with sharp insight, his characterization is one of the most powerful in the epic, and has remained as such in popular imagination to this day.

The tragedy of Karna begins with Kunti, the mother of the three elder Pandava princes. While still unmarried, she received a magic boon which enabled her to have children from the gods. After her husband, Pandu, became incapable of procreation she made use of the boon to have three sons from the gods to continue his line, and also helped his other wife, Madri, to have two more sons similarly. These five brothers were legally and socially accepted as the Pandava princes. But, unknown to them, they also had an elder half-brother. This was Karna illegitimately born from the sun-god to Kunti before her marriage and abandoned by her in shame.

Karna was found by a humble chariot-driver and his wife Radha who brought him up as their own child. The stigma of supposed low birth dogged him through most of his life. Despite his superlative qualities he was humiliated and rebuffed: in trying to learn the martial arts from the teacher of the Kauravas and the Pandavas; in challenging Arjuna in a military tournament; and in sueing for the hand of the princess Draupadi. Duryodhana gave him status by making him the king of Anga, and won in turn his lasting loyalty and friendship. But his continued hankering for acceptance made him haughty, conscious of status, and anxious to cultivate a reputation for charity to an excessive degree.

His obsessive rivalry with Arjuna was another influence on Karna. In its pursuit he obtained divine weapons from the sage Parashu Rama by dissimulation, only to be told that they would fail him at the critical moment. On the other hand, out of pride, he gave away his own divine armour to the king of the gods, disguised as a supplicant, even though he knew that this was a trick to weaken him in the eventual conflict with Arjuna. In turn he received an infallible weapon which he expended against Ghatotkacha to protect Duryodhana's army.

Before the commencement of the war both Krishna and Kunti tell Karna about his actual parentage and invite him to change sides. Krishna tells him that as the eldest son of Kunti he would become the acknowledged ruler of the Pandava kingdom. But Karna remains steadfast in his loyalty to Duryodhana. He promises Kunti that he would fight to the end only with Arjuna.

In a gesture of high nobility he asks Krishna not to reveal the secret of his birth to the Pandavas, for then they would feel obliged to give him the kingdom which, in turn, he would be bound to present to Duryodhana. He adds that in his heart he knows that virtue and victory lie on the side of the Pandavas.

In the epic Karna is tricked by Indra to donate his armour before the war begins. In the play this happens on the battlefield. The other character in the play is Shalya. An uncle of the Pandavas, in the epic, he agrees to become Karna's charioteer with a secret understanding that he will do his best to demoralize him when he engages Arjuna in battle. There are, accordingly, lengthy recriminations between him and Karna in the epic. In the play, however, he appears as a wise supporter and adviser.

Cast in order of appearance

Producer	*in the Prologue*
A Soldier	*of the Kaurava army in the war against the Pandavas*
Karna	*King of Anga, commander of the Kaurava army*
Shalya	*A king and Kaurava commander, charioteer of Karna*
Indra	*king of the gods, partisan of the Pandavas*
Angel	*messenger of Indra*

Other characters mentioned in the play

Duryodhana	*chief of the Kauravas*
Arjuna	*the third Pandava, rival and eventual slayer of Karna*
Kunti	*mother of the Pandavas, and illegitimately of Karna*
Radha	*Karna's adoptive mother*

Prologue

[After the benediction, enter the Producer]

PRODUCER May he bless you all, that destroyer of demons at whose form, half-man half-lion, the whole world marvelled, even as he pierced the demon king's breast with his sharp adamantine claws. And now, distinguished spectators, I have to announce that—but what is that? There seems to be a sound just as I was about to start. Well, let me see.

[Voice off stage]

VOICE Ho there! Let it be known! Let it be known to His Majesty the lord of Anga. . . .

PRODUCER Ah, I see. The tumult of battle has commenced and, on the instructions of Duryodhana, a soldier informs Karna about it excitedly, with hands joined in salute.

[Exit]

[END OF PROLOGUE]

ACT I

[Enter a Soldier]

SOLDIER Ho there! Let it be known! Let it be known to His Majesty the lord of Anga that the battle is at hand. Exultant princes on their elephants, horses and chariots roar like lions under Arjuna's banner. And, in response, the irresistible elephant-standard of the Kaurava king swiftly moves into the battlefield. (*Moves about and looks*) Ah! There is the king of Anga, attired for battle, emerging from his palace with King Shalya. But what is that shadow on his face, unprecedented in one whose valour is known to all, one who has always been the leader in the festival of war? This wise and powerful warrior seems overtaken by some sadness. It is as if the natural brilliance of the mid-summer sun were to be dimmed by unseasonal clouds. Well, let me go. (*Exit*)

[Enter Karna, as described, with Shalya]

KARNA The warriors on whom I aim my arrows have never escaped. I would fulfil the Kauravas' desire if I could meet Arjuna in the battlefield.

King Shalya, drive my chariot towards Arjuna, wherever he is.

SHALYA Very well.

KARNA Why do I feel bereft at this time of battle? I, who am like an angry god of death in combat, smashing enemies in the clash of arms? Is it because I am the firstborn of Kunti, but known as the son of Radha? Is it because Yudhishthira and the other Pandavas are my younger brothers? This day of reckoning has at last arrived. But my skill with weapons seems worthless, and I am also restrained by my mother. O King Shalya, hear the story of my weapons.

SHALYA I am indeed curious to hear this tale.

KARNA In the beginning I had gone to Parashu Rama.

SHALYA And then?

KARNA That sage had destroyed the warrior caste. His hair was the colour of a lightning flash. His battleaxe shone with a halo of light. I saluted him and stood still.

SHALYA And then?

KARNA Then Parashu Rama blessed me. And he asked me: 'Who are you, why have you come?'

SHALYA And then?

KARNA I said: 'Lord, I wish to learn all the skills of weapons.'

SHALYA And then?

KARNA Then he replied: 'I teach scholars; I do not teach those of the warrior caste.'

SHALYA Of course he had an old enmity with the warriors. And then?

KARNA Then I said I am not of the warrior caste; and I began to learn the skills of weapons from him.

SHALYA And then?

KARNA After some time had passed, I once went with the sage to collect fruit and flowers and firewood.

SHALYA And then?

KARNA The sage got tired from wandering in the forest. He reclined in my lap and fell asleep.

SHALYA And then?

KARNA Then by chance the insect called thunder mouth bit me in the thighs. I did not want to disturb my teacher's sleep, so I quietly bore that excruciating pain. But my bleeding wet him also, and he woke up. Recognizing me for what I was, he suddenly flared with anger and cursed that my weapons may fail me in time of need.

SHALYA O that was a dreadful thing to say.

KARNA So, let us test this tale of the weapons. (*Does so*) These weapons seem as if they have lost their force. And so do these horses, with their downcast eyes and desperate, faltering gait. And those rutting elephants with their forest smells seem to ask that we turn back from battle. The drums and bugles of war have also become silent.

SHALYA O this is terrible indeed.

KARNA But enough of despondency, King Shalya. If we die, we attain heaven. If we win, we obtain fame. Both are worthwhile. War is not worthless.

And these fine Kabul horses, swift as eagles and every ready for battle, may they protect me, as I protect them. Long live the holy priests and cows. Long live the virtuous women. Long live the brave soldiers. And long live I, whose moment has come. Now I am content. I will enter this difficult battle with the Pandavas. Capturing Yudhishthira, famous for his virtues, and felling Arjuna with the force of my excellent arrows, I will make this battlefield as tranquil as a forest when the lion is killed. King Shalya, let us mount the chariot.

SHALYA Very well. (*Both mount the chariot*)

KARNA King Shalya, drive my chariot towards Arjuna, wherever he is.

[Voice off stage]

VOICE O Karna, give me something big!

KARNA (*Listening*) That is a powerful voice! Its deep tone has suddenly brought these horses of mine to a dead halt. They stand transfixed as if in a picture, ears cocked, necks arched, eyes unblinking. That is not just a priest. He has majesty. Call him. No, no. I will call him myself. This way, sir, this way.

[Enter Indra in the guise of a priest]

INDRA O clouds, you may go back together with the sun. (*Approaching Karna*) O Karna, give me something big!

KARNA I am very pleased, sir. Many crowned heads have bowed at my feet. But today I consider myself fortunate to be able to bow at the feet of an Indra among priests. Sir, Karna salutes you.

INDRA (*To himself*) Now, what should I say in return? If I say the customary 'May you live long,' he will have a long life. If I say nothing, he will consider me a churl. These aside, what shall I do? (*To Karna*) O Karna! May thy fame live long, like the sun, like the moon, like the mountains, like the sea.

KARNA Sir, shouldn't you say 'live long'? But this also is befitting. Power flits like the serpent's tongue. Virtue alone is worth striving for. Kings live on through their virtues when they die. What do you want, sir? What should I give?

INDRA Give me something big.

KARNA I will give you something big indeed. Hear what I have, priest. I will give you a thousand cows, young, desirable, with milk like nectar and sturdy calves, with horns trimmed in pure gold.

INDRA A thousand cows? To drink a bit of milk? No, Karna, I don't want them.

KARNA You don't want them? Listen again. I will give you this very moment a thousand Kabul horses, swift as the wind, tested in war, excellent like the sun's own stallions.

INDRA Horses? To ride for a moment? No, Karna, I don't want them.

KARNA You don't want them? Well, listen once more. I will give you a herd of rutting war-elephants, splendid like mountains, with white tusks and voices like thunder.

INDRA Elephants? To ride for a moment? No, Karna, I don't want them.

KARNA You don't want them either? Then I will give you all the gold you can want.

INDRA I'll take it and go. (*Goes some distance*) No, Karna, I don't want it.

KARNA Then I will conquer the earth and give it to you.

INDRA What will I do with the earth?

KARNA Then I will give you the fruit of the holy sacrifice.

INDRA What's the use of the sacrificial fruit?

KARNA Then take my head!

INDRA Heaven protect me!

KARNA Don't be frightened, don't be frightened please, sir. Listen again. I was born with this protective armour. It is a part of my body. It is impenetrable by god or demon. If it pleases you, I will gladly give it to you.

INDRA (*Happily*) Give it! Give it!

KARNA (*To himself*) So this was his purpose. This must be a stratagem of that cunning Krishna. So be it. But I should not think thus. There is no cause for doubt. (*To Indra*) Take it.

SHALYA King of Anga, do not give it, do not give it.

KARNA Do not stop me, King Shalya. Look, in the course of time strong trees fall and lakes go dry, even knowledge perishes. What remains for ever is the merit of sacrificing and of giving. So, take it. (*Takes off and gives the armour*).

INDRA (*Taking it, to himself*) So, I have it. I have already done what I had promised before all the gods for Arjuna's victory. Now I will mount my elephant and watch the duel between Karna and Arjuna. (*Exit*)

SHALYA O king of Anga! Your Majesty has been tricked.

KARNA By whom?

SHALYA By Indra.

KARNA No, indeed. Indra has been tricked by me. Because that wearer of the crown and receiver of holy sacrifices, that destroyer of demons and rider of celestial elephants, has now become my debtor.

[Enter an angel disguised as a priest]

ANGEL O Karna, you have been rewarded by Indra who feels remorse at having taken your armour. Take this irresistible weapon called Vimala for slaying anyone among the Pandava brothers.

KARNA Shame! I do not accept anything in return for my gift.

ANGEL Please accept the request of a priest.

KARNA The request of a priest? I have never refused one. When will I get it?

ANGEL Call for it in your mind, and you will have the weapon.

KARNA Very well. I am grateful. You may return, sir.

ANGEL Very well. (*Exit*)

KARNA King Shalya, let us mount the chariot.

SHALYA Very well.

[Both mount the chariot]

KARNA O what is that sound? It is the blast of a conch-shell, deep as the ocean's roar in the final deluge. Perhaps by Krishna or by Arjuna. Angry at Yudhishthira's defeat, Arjuna will certainly fight at his best today. King Shalya, drive my chariot towards Arjuna, wherever he is.

SHALYA Very well.

Epilogue

May there be prosperity everywhere.
May all difficulties disappear.
May a king with kingly virtues,
Rule us on this land united.

[Exit all]

The Shattered Thigh

Urubhangam

{6}

The Shattered Thigh

Urubhangam

The last great battle of the Mahābhārata war was a duel with maces between the Kaurava chief Duryodhana and the Pandava prince Bhima, which ended with the former's defeat and death.

As described in the ninth book of the epic, this final clash took place in the presence of the other four Pandava princes, as well as Krishna and his brother Balarama. Duryodhana was alone. In the beginning the combat did not go well for Bhima. Krishna told Arjuna that it would not be possible to defeat Duryodhana in a fair fight and, at his urging, Arjuna signalled to Bhima that he should aim for his opponent's thigh. This was a foul blow according to the rules of combat with maces. But Bhima executed it and shattered Duryodhana's thigh. He then abused the fallen Duryodhana, and in turn was censured by Balarama for using unfair means. Krishna defended Bhima, but Balarama was not convinced and left the scene after praising Duryodhana. The Pandavas and Krishna also departed after some heated words with the mortally wounded but still defiant Duryodhana.

While Krishna and the Pandavas were consoling Duryodhana's parents, the blind Dhritarashtra and queen Gandhari, at their palace, Duryodhana was visited by the few remaining Kaurava warriors. One of them was Ashwatthama, the son of the royal preceptor Drona who had earlier perished in the war. Greatly moved to see the once mighty Duryodhana lying defeated, Ashwatthama swore that he would destroy the Pandavas. Duryodhana promptly consecrated him as his next commander-in-chief. The tenth book of the epic narrates Ashwatthama's nocturnal attack on the Pandava camp and the subsequent death of Duryodhana.

In the present play these events are described in a compressed form. Departing from the epic, the playwright creates his own dramatic effect by bringing Duryodhana's parents to his side together with his two queens and a young son. The latter does not figure in the epic at all.

The play is also remarkable for its tragic ending, and for the depiction of Duryodhana's death on stage, in breach of the classic conventions of Sanskrit dramaturgy. On the other hand, it adheres to the convention of not depicting warfare on stage. The duel between Bhima and Duryodhana is, instead, vividly described in an opening interlude through a chorus of three soldiers, comparable to the three priests describing the sacrificial ceremony in *Five Nights*.

Duryodhana is the central figure is this play. In turn defiant or resigned, vindictive or forgiving, despairing or proud, his characterization here completes the portrait earlier outlined in *Five Nights, The Envoy* and *The Message*. An additional touch is given by the poignant encounter of the dying Duryodhana with his wives and his son.

This play, again of the type *anka* evoking the heroic and the compassionate flavours, is probably the nearest to a tragedy in the modern sense that exists in classical Sanskrit literature.

Cast in order of appearance

The Producer	*in the Prologue*
His assistant	*in the Prologue*
Three Soldiers	*of the Kaurava army*
Balarama	*elder brother of Krishna*
Duryodhana	*chief of the Kauravas, eldest son of Dhritarashtra*
Dhritarashtra	*the blind old king*
Gandhari	*wife of Dhritarashtra*
Malavi	*wife of Duryodhana*
Pauravi	*wife of Duryodhana*
Durjaya	*young son of Duryodhana*
Ashwatthama	*son of the Kurus' preceptor*
Other characters mentioned in the play	
Vyasa	*a famous sage*
Vidura	*a half-brother of Dhritarashtra*

Prologue

[After the benediction, enter the Producer]

PRODUCER May Krishna help you surmount your enemies. The same, who took Arjuna across the flooded river of his foes. A river whose source was Shakuni, and the torrent Duryodhana. A river full of swords and arrows, with Jayadratha as the water and Karna as the waves, with Bhishma and Drona as its two banks, and with Ashwatthama and Kripa as lurking crocodiles. And now, distinguished spectators, I have to announce that—but what is that? There seems to be a sound just as I was about to start. Well, let me look.

[Voices off stage]

VOICES We are here! Sir, we are here!

PRODUCER Ah, I see.

[Enter an Assistant]

ASSISTANT Sir, from where have these people come? Their limbs are wounded with thrusts of spears and arrows and elephant tusks. They challenge each other as they rush about. It seems they want to die fighting for the sake of glory.

PRODUCER Don't you understand, sir? Kurukshetra is littered with the corpses of kings. Only Duryodhana remains on the side of blind Dhritarashtra who has already lost a hundred sons. And on the side of Yudhishthira, only Krishna and the Pandava brothers remain. The battlefield is like one of those pictures, full of minute details. Dead elephants and horses, dead kings and soldiers, all killed in combat. And the combat of Bhima and Duryodhana is about to begin. Their warriors are already dead.

[Exit]

[END OF PROLOGUE]

ACT I

[Enter three soldiers]

ALL We are here! Sir, we are here!

FIRST This is war. The cauldron of hate and brute force, of pride and glory. Where the nymphs of heaven select their bridegrooms. Where lives are sacrificed, and princes find heroic deathbeds and stairways to paradise.

SECOND That's right. The ground is dotted with dead elephants. There are nesting vultures and empty chariots on all sides. The princes are no more. Yet, they still live, such were their deeds in battle.

THIRD Quite so. War is a sacred sacrifice. Enmity fans its flames. Elephant trunks are the ritual posts, and arrows the ceremonial grass. Men perish there as sacrificial beasts. Their cries are the sacred chants.

FIRST Look this side, gentlemen. These nobles lie dead here, struck by each others' shafts. And those birds with bloodstained beaks are trying to loosen the ornaments from their bodies.

SECOND And that war-elephant fallen under a hail of darts, its armour pierced. It looks like an arsenal with all the bows and arrows around it.

THIRD And there's another sight. Those jackals are eagerly pulling out a dead warrior from his chariot, with all his jewelled quiver and garlands. From the same chariot, would his sisters-in-law have helped him down when he was a bridegroom.

ALL Kurukshetra is a terrifying sight today. The ground is a slush with the blood of elephants, horses and men. Broken armour and all kinds of weapons are scattered everywhere.

FIRST Dead elephants lie like bridges in pools of blood. Others wander crazed, without their drivers. Horses pull empty chariots. Headless trunks writhe and twitch.

SECOND Look at those vultures with wings outstretched, like palm-leaf fans in the sky. They have pale eyes, and beaks like elephant goads, with bits of flesh on them like coral.

THIRD All these dead horses and elephants, soldiers and chieftains are so sharply etched by the harsh glare of sunlight. And so are the scattered spears and arrows, swords and daggers. Like stars fallen on the earth.

FIRST But even in this condition, the warriors look splendid. Their fearless faces are still like lotuses, lying on land.

SECOND Even such warriors cannot resist death, what to say of lesser people.

THIRD Death is the soldier's fate.

FIRST Without doubt.

SECOND That's not so. It was Arjuna who forced death on these proud chiefs, with his sharp arrows and terrible bow.

ALL Listen, there's a sound. The rumble of a thundercloud? A thunderbolt on a mountain peak? A tremor in the earth below? The crash of waves in a stormy sea? Let's see.

[All move around]

FIRST Look! The combat between Bhima and Duryodhana has begun. The middle Pandava is incensed, remembering the humiliation of Draupadi. The king is enraged at the killing of his hundred brothers. They are duelling with maces before Vyasa and Vidura, Krishna and Balarama, and the other Kuru and Yadava leaders.

SECOND Bhima's broad chest is like a golden rock. Duryodhana's shoulders are hard as an elephant's trunk. They strike at each other with weapons poised. That sound is the clash of their maces.

THIRD Look at the king! His face is flushed with anger. His helmet plume quivers as he advances crouching, his arm extended. The blood-spattered mace in his right hand gleams like lightning on Mount Kailasa.

FIRST Look at Bhima. His body is covered with blood. It flows from his gashed brow and shoulders. His chest is wet with gouts of blood. Wounded and bleeding from mace blows, he looks like a mountain covered with streams of red mud.

SECOND Duryodhana swings a fearful mace. He roars as he springs. He is quick to draw his arm and ward the other's blow. He advances striking relentlessly. The king has more skill. But Bhima is stronger.

THIRD Bhima is like a mountain. He has no match in a fight. But he is wet with blood from that big wound on his head. And look! He has fallen down! Like a mountain peak struck by lightning.

FIRST Bhimasena has fallen! His legs buckled under that heavy blow. Vyasa seems astonished, his face upturned resting on a single finger under the chin.

SECOND Yudhishthira looks distressed. Vidura is in tears.

THIRD Arjuna plucks at his bow, Gandiva. Krishna stares at the sky.

ALL Balarama is waving his plough with excitement. He loves his pupil.

FIRST The king is brave. His helmet gleams with gems. He is radiant with daring, with dignity and arrogance. He says mockingly: 'Don't be afraid, Bhima. The brave do not strike someone who is down during battle!'

SECOND Seeing Bhimasena thus ridiculed, Krishna now gives him a sign, striking his own thighs.

THIRD That sign seems to have assured Bhima. Seeing his son's distress, the wind-god has also given him strength. He knits his brow, wipes off the sweat, and grasps his mace 'Chitrangada' with both hands. Then, roaring like a lion at a bull, he stands up again.

FIRST Oh! The combat has started again. The son of Pandu rubs his hands on the ground, bites his lip and roars with rage. But that's a foul! He follows Krishna's sign, but ignores the rules. With a swift and deep two-handed swing he has hurled the mace on the thighs of Gandhari's son!

ALL Alas! The king has fallen.

THIRD Seeing the king fallen, his body pale with loss of blood, the blessed Vyasa has risen into the sky. Balarama covers his eyes. He is angry for Duryodhana. Meanwhile, on Vyasa's advice, Krishna and the Pandavas lead Bhima away.

FIRST Bhimasena's departure has been noticed by Balarama, even though his eyes were closed. Balarama's headdress quivers. His eyes are bloodshot with anger. As he pulls up his garland and draws his dark garment around his body, he looks like the moon descended on earth.

SECOND Come, let us also go and attend on the king.

THE OTHERS Very good.

[Exit all]

ACT II

[Enter Balarama]

BALARAMA That was not fair, O you kings. He cheated in the contest. He was too proud to care about me or my death-dealing plough. In open battle he brought the mace down on Duryodhana's thighs, and also dragged down the reputation of his own family. Live on, Duryodhana! Till I plunge this plough into Bhima's breast today, and make it full of furrows wet with sweat and blood.

[Voice off stage]

VOICE Please! Please, lord Balarama!

BALARAMA O poor Duryodhana! Even in this plight he follows me. Like a child he drags himself on the ground. His arms are pale with dust. His body is smeared and wet with the bloody cosmetic of war. But he is splendid, like the serpent dragging its tired body through the water, after having been used to churn the ocean.

[Enter Duryodhana, with both his thighs broken]

DURYODHANA Here I am. Bhima broke the rules of war. His mace blow shattered my thighs. I drag my half-dead body along the earth with my arms. But please, lord Balarama, please calm your anger. Today, for the first time, this head is on the ground, at your feet. We are finished. And so is the war and the enmity. Now just let the funeral of the Kuru clan proceed.

BALARAMA O Duryodhana, live on, at least for a little while.

DURYODHANA What are you going to do?

BALARAMA Listen. I will make an offering for your fallen comrades. I will give them the sons of Pandu, their bodies pierced with my plough and smashed with my club.

DURYODHANA No, no, sir. Bhima fulfilled his vow. My brothers have gone to heaven. I am in this condition. What will be achieved by fighting?

BALARAMA Sir, you were cheated before my eyes. That has made me very angry.

DURYODHANA You think I was cheated?

BALARAMA Is there any doubt about it?

DURYODHANA O I had put my life on stake. Bhima had the wit to escape from that dreadful fire in the house of lac. He survived the avalanche of rocks in the battle with Kubera. He killed the demon Hidimba. If you think, Balarama, that he beat me today by deceit, that is just not so.

BALARAMA Should Bhimasena live, having cheated you in battle?

DURYODHANA Was I cheated by Bhimasena?

BALARAMA Then by whom have you been brought to this pass?

DURYODHANA Listen. Who defied Indra and took away the wishing tree from paradise? Who sleeps for sport on the ocean for a thousand celestial years? Who is the world's beloved? It was he who suddenly entered Bhima's sharp mace and delivered me to death.

[Voices off stage]

VOICES Move aside, gentlemen, move aside!

BALARAMA (*Looking*) Oh! That is His Majesty Dhritarashtra with Gandhari, led by Durjaya. The ladies of the inner palace are also with him. His step falters. His heart is full of grief. But it is also full of courage. The gods were fearful at his birth, and blinded him. He distributed his sight among a hundred sons. He still stands proud and upright. His long arms are like columns of gold.

[Enter Dhritarashtra, Gandhari, two Queens and Durjaya]

DHRITARASHTRA My son, where are you?

GANDHARI Where are you, my child?

QUEENS Great king, where are you?

DHRITARASHTRA Alas! My sightless eyes have been blinded even more by tears since I heard today that my son had been struck down by trickery. Gandhari, are you there?

GANDHARI Alas! I am still alive.

QUEENS Great king! O great king!

DURYODHANA Alas! My wives are also weeping. I had hardly noticed the mace's blow before. It is only now that I feel its full force, when my women come into the battlefield with their heads uncovered.

DHRITARASHTRA Gandhari, can you see Duryodhana, the pride of our family?

GANDHARI I cannot see him, Your Majesty.

DHRITARASHTRA What do you mean? Alas, today I am truly blind, when I cannot even see my son at this time of need. I was the proud father of a hundred splendid sons. Do I not deserve that even one should remain to make my funeral offering?

GANDHARI Suyodhana, my boy, answer me. Say something to console your grief-stricken father.

BALARAMA That is queen Gandhari. She always yearned to see her children and grand-children, but kept her eyes bandaged out of devotion to her husband. Now even her fortitude is overcome by grief. That bandage of devotion is wet with tears.

DHRITARASHTRA Duryodhana! My son! King of eighteen armies! Where are you?

DURYODHANA A king indeed today!

DHRITARASHTRA My firstborn son! Come! Answer me!

DURYODHANA Answer you indeed! I am ashamed at what has happened.

DHRITARASHTRA Come, my son, greet me.

DURYODHANA I am coming. (*Tries to get up, but falls again*) Alas! This is the second blow. Bhimasena's mace has today deprived me, both of using my thighs and of saluting my father.

GANDHARI Here, my daughters.

QUEENS We are here, madam.

GANDHARI Go to your husband.

QUEENS We go, ill-fated as we are.

DHRITARASHTRA Who is this guiding me? Tugging at the hem of my garment?

DURJAYA It's me, grandfather. Durjaya.

DHRITARASHTRA Durjaya! Go, grandson, look to your father.

DURJAYA But I am tired, grandfather.

DHRITARASHTRA Go, rest in your father's lap.

DURJAYA I am going. (*Approaching*) Father, where are you?

DURYODHANA Oh, he has come too. Love for a son is always in one's heart. In all conditions. But now it burns me. Durjaya has never known sorrow. He has only known the comfort of his father's lap. What will he say when he sees me defeated?

DURJAYA Here's the great king. He's sitting on the ground.

DURYODHANA My son! Why have you come?

DURJAYA You were away for so long.

DURYODHANA Ah! Even in this condition, love for my son burns my heart.

DURJAYA I want to sit in your lap. (*Tries to climb on to Duryodhana's thighs*)

DURYODHANA (*Preventing him*) Durjaya! Durjaya! The pain! Alas! This light of my eyes, delight of my heart, this moon, is now a burning fire.

DURJAYA Why don't you let me sit in your lap?

DURYODHANA Let it be, my son. Sit anywhere else. From today your old familiar sitting place is not there any more.

DURJAYA Why, where is the great king going?

DURYODHANA I am going to my brothers.

DURJAYA Take me there also.

DURYODHANA Tell that to Bhima, my son.

DURJAYA Come, great king, you are being called.

DURYODHANA By whom, son?

DURJAYA By Her Majesty and His Majesty and all the palace ladies.

DURYODHANA You go, my son. I cannot come.

DURJAYA I'll take you.

DURYODHANA You are still too small, my son.

DURJAYA (*Walking around*) Ladies, the great king is here.

QUEENS The great king! Alas! Alas!

DHRITARASHTRA Where is the great king?

GANDHARI Where is my child?

DURJAYA Here he is, sitting on the ground.

DHRITARASHTRA Alas! Is this the great king? He was like a pillar of gold, the king of all kings. And now my poor boy lies on the floor, like a broken doorpost.

GANDHARI Suyodhana, my child. You must be tired.

DURYODHANA My lady, I am your son.

DHRITARASHTRA Who is that?

GANDHARI It is I, great king, who gave birth to fearless sons.

DURYODHANA I now feel reborn today. Come father, why this distress now?

DHRITARASHTRA Why would I be distressed, son? Your hundred brave brothers were consecrated for battle. They have all perished. With you, I also am dead. (*Falls*)

DURYODHANA Alas! His Majesty has fallen. Father, you must console the queen.

DHRITARASHTRA What consolation can I give her?

DURYODHANA Say I died in battle facing the foe. O father, control your grief for my sake. I have bowed my head only at your feet. I have no care for this fire raging within me. I will go to heaven just as proudly as I was born.

DHRITARASHTRA I am old and blind from birth. I have no wish to live. And now this bitter grief for my children has come upon me.

BALARAMA Alas! His eyes are closed for ever. He has lost all hope for his son. I can hardly announce myself to him just now.

DURYODHANA My lady, I would like to say something to you.

GANDHARI Speak, my child.

DURYODHANA With folded hands I say to you, if I have done any good at all in this life, be my mother in my future lives also.

GANDHARI You speak indeed my own wish.

DURYODHANA Malavi, you also listen. Blows of the mace have bloodied my brow. The blood on my breast leaves no place for garlands. Look at my arms, with wounds as fine as golden bracelets. But your husband fell in battle without turning his back. You are a warrior's wife. Why should you weep?

MALAVI I am just a girl, your wedded wife. So I weep.

DURYODHANA And you, Pauravi. We performed the various sacrifices enjoined by the scriptures. We looked after the family. Our dependents had no complaints. Our dear brothers subjugated the enemies. The kings of the eighteen armies were given a hard battle. You are a proud woman. Think of my pride. Wives of such men do not weep.

PAURAVI I have already decided to go with you. So I do not weep.

DURYODHANA Durjaya, you listen also.

DHRITARASHTRA Gandhari, what does he say?

GANDHARI My own thoughts.

DURYODHANA You must listen to the Pandavas just as you do to me. Obey the orders of the lady, mother Kunti. Honour Draupadi and the mother of Abhimanyu like your own mother. Look, my son! Duryodhana was your father. He was splendid and glorious. His heart was fired with pride. He fell in battle facing an equal adversary. Just remember this and give up grief. Then, touching the silk on Yudhishthira's strong right arm, you must join the sons of Pandu in offering the funeral water in my name.

BALARAMA Ah! Enmity gives way to remorse. Well, the drums and trumpets are silent. Arrows and armour, fans and umbrellas, all lie scattered. The soldiers and charioteers all lie dead. But there is a noise. Frightened crows are wheeling in the sky. From whose bow is that sound?

[Ashwatthama's voice off stage]

ASHWATTHAMA I came to this battle with Duryodhana when he raised the bow. I was as eager as a priest coming to the great horse sacrifice. Now I have come again.

BALARAMA Oh, that is the preceptor's son coming here. Ashwatthama. Large, clear eyes. Long golden arms. Angrily drawing that terrible bow. He shines like Mount Meru with a rainbow on its peak.

[Enter Ashwatthama]

ASHWATTHAMA Listen to me, you warrior kings. Your armies came together in battle like two oceans. Like sharks were the upraised weapons. Few survive, and their life ebbs with each breath. But it was the Kuru king, not I, whose thighs were shattered by deceit. It was the charioteer's son, not I, whose weapons failed. Today, I, the son of Drona, stand alone on this field of victory, my weapons drawn. But, for me also, what is the point of glory in war without the accolade of victory. (*Walking around*) But, no. The king of the Kurus was cheated when I was busy with my father's funeral. Who will believe it? The lords of eleven armies waited with folded hands upon his words. Bhishma and my father fought for him in the battle. It is clear that Duryodhana was defeated only by bad luck. Now where is he? (*Walking around and looking*) Ah! Here is the Kuru king. He has crossed the ocean of war, and now lies in the midst of fallen elephants and horses, chariots and soldiers. His hair is dishevelled. His limbs are wet with blood from mace blows. He lies on this final stony seat, like the sun at sunset, sinking into twilight. (*Approaching him*) O Kuru king, what is this?

DURYODHANA The fruit of craving, O son of my teacher.

ASHWATTHAMA Your Majesty, I am going to put aside the proprieties.

DURYODHANA What are you going to do?

ASHWATTHAMA Krishna wants to fight. I am going to wipe out the sons of Pandu, together with him and his eagle and discus. Like bad lines from a drawing.

DURYODHANA No. No, sir, not that. All those crowned kings are no more. Karna has gone to heaven. Bhishma has fallen. All my hundred brothers have perished in battle. And we are in this condition. Lay down your bow, sir.

ASHWATTHAMA Your Majesty, it seems that in the contest when Bhima struck you with the mace and seized you by the hair, he crushed your pride and spirit also, along with your thighs.

DURYODHANA No, no. What are kings but pride. It was for the sake of pride that I chose this war. Look, teacher's son, how Draupadi was dragged by the hair at the gambling match, how Abhimanyu was killed in battle while still a boy, how the Pandavas were beaten by a trick of the dice and sent to live in the forest with wild animals. Just think, there is not much they have done to break my spirit and pride.

ASHWATTHAMA I swear by everything, by you, by the paradise of warriors, by my own soul, I will attack tonight and destroy the Pandavas in battle.

BALARAMA This will certainly happen. The preceptor's son has said it.

ASHWATTHAMA Lord Balarama.

DHRITARASHTRA Alas, this conspiracy has a witness.

ASHWATTHAMA Come here, Durjaya. By this priest's oath, may you be the uncrowned king of all the realm won by your father's strength and valour.

DURYODHANA Bless you! What my heart wanted is done. Now my life is going. Shantanu and all my royal ancestors are here. Here are my brothers with Karna at their head. Here too is Abhimanyu, with his boyish tresses, sitting on Indra's elephant, berating me angrily. Urvashi and the celestial nymphs have come to receive me. Here are the oceans, and the Ganga and the other rivers. Death has sent a warrior's car drawn by a thousand swans to fetch me. I come. (*Dies*)

[He is covered with a cloth]

DHRITARASHTRA Curse this kingdom, useless with the death of my sons. I go to the forest hermitage where decent people live.

ASHWATTHAMA And I go, weapon in hand, ready to kill those who sleep tonight.

Benediction

BALARAMA May the lord of men destroy the enemies and protect us all.

[Exit all]

Notes to Introduction

1. P.S. Sane, G.H. Godbole and H.S. Ursekar, eds., *Mālavikāgnimitra of Kalidasa*, Bombay, 1950. This, and the other translations in the introduction are by A.N.D. Haksar.
2. Original quoted in introduction to *Subhāshitavali*, ed., R.D. Karmarkar, *Bombay Sanskrit & Prakrit Series*, Poona, 1961.
3. ibid.
4. ibid.
5. ibid.
6. ibid., verse 1821.
7. ibid., verse 1994.
8. T.G. Sastri, *Bhasa's Works*, Trivandrum, 1925.
9. cf. C.R. Devadhar, *Plays ascribed to Bhasa: Their Authenticity and Merits*, Poona, 1927; A.K. Warder, *Indian Kavya Literature*, Vol. II, Delhi, 1974; R.N. Saletore, *Encyclopaedia of Indian Culture*, New Delhi, Vol. I, 1981, *Bhāsanātakachakram*, introduction by Acharya Baladeva Upadhyaya, Chowkhamba Vidya Bhavan, Varanasi; *A Cultural History of India*, ed., A.L. Basham, Oxford University Press, 1975.
10. e.g. A.D. Pusalker, *Bhasa—A Study*, Lahore, 1940.
11. *Thirteen Plays of Bhasa*, trans., A.C. Woolner & L. Sarup, Punjab University, Oriental Publications, No. 13, 1930.
12. R.N. Saletore, *Encyclopaedia of Indian Culture*, New Delhi, Vol. I, 1981. The verse in question is found in *Pratijnā Yaugardharāyana*, IV. 2 and in *Arthaśāstra*, X. 3.

13. Included in *A Cultural History of India*, ed., A.L. Basham, Oxford University Press, 1975, cf. articles by Romila Thapar and A.K. Warder in the same, for this section.
14. *Nātysāstra*, Chowkhamba, Varanasi, 1926; cf. also S.C. Bhatt, *Drama in Ancient India*, New Delhi, 1961; and *Indian Literature*, Sanskrit literature number, Sahitya Akademi, New Delhi, 1978, for this section.
15. Introduction by Dr Suniti Kumar Chatterji to *Indian Drama*, Publications Division, New Delhi, 1956.
16. Original quoted in introduction to *Mālavikāgnimitra of Kalidasa*, eds., P.S. Sane, G.H. Godbole and H.S. Ursekar, Bombay, 1950.
17. M.L. Varadpande, *Religion and Theatre*, New Delhi, 1983.
18. cf. *Thirteen Plays of Bhasa*, trans, A.C. Woolner and L. Sarup, Punjab University, Oriental Publications, No. 13, 1930, for this section.
19. The critical edition of the *Mahaābhārata* was ed. by V.S. Sukthankar and others, Bhandarkar Oriental Research Institute, Poona, 1925–70. A well-known English translation is by J.A.B. Van Buitenen, University of Chicago Press, 1973–78. There are numerous retold versions; cf. also the *Mahābhārata, a Literary Study*, by Krishna Chaitanya, New Delhi, 1985; *Moral Dilemmas in the Mahābhārata*, ed., B.K. Matilal, Indian Institute of Advanced Study, Shimla, 1989; *The Book of Yudhisthir*, Buddhadeva Bose, Hyderabad, 1986.